A Café in Space

The Anaïs Nin Literary Journal

Sky Blue Press
San Antonio, Texas

Front Cover:
Anaïs Nin, 1960s. Photo: Christian Dubois Larson.

Back Cover:
"Cracked Actress." Mixed media by Colette Standish.

Social media

Blog: http://anaisninblog.skybluepress.com

Twitter: @anaisninblog

Table of Contents

Volume 14 2017

Edited by **Paul Herron**

Acknowledgments

The Editor would like to thank the following for their assistance in the realization of this issue:

The Anaïs Nin Trust for permissions to use quotations from Anaïs Nin and for photographic material.

Sara Herron, without whom none of this would be possible.

Agape Editions for a review copy of *Anaïs Nin: An Unprofessional Study.*

A Café in Space: the Anaïs Nin Literary Journal is published annually by Sky Blue Press and is edited by Paul Herron. We welcome submissions of articles or proposals having to do with Anaïs Nin and her circle.

Our website, found at www.skybluepress.com, allows users to browse the contents of past issues of this publication. Our blog (http://anaisninblog.skybluepress.com) is a place where readers can keep up to date on events and publications concerning Anaïs Nin, and you can follow us on Twitter (@anaisninblog). It is our sincere hope that with the journal, blog and website we will be able to form a "café" in which Nin scholars, readers, and those with parallel interests will gather. Nin study is hampered by a lack of communication between those of us who engage in it, and this is a way to address the problem. We encourage you to "spread the word" so that we can build a strong, interconnected community of Nin scholarship and readership.

Submissions or proposals should be attached as Word documents and directed to skybluepress@skybluepress.com. Please identify the contents in the subject line or they will not be opened. E-mail us if you wish information about how to send materials through the mail. Any unsolicited material will not be returned without inclusion of a self-stamped and self-addressed envelope. Saftey of manuscripts and other materials is not the responsibility of Sky Blue Press.

ISBN: 9780-9987246-1-4

Editor's Note

The coming year looms large for Anaïs Nin's canon as we await the publication of her fifth unexpurgated diary, one that is perhaps more anticipated than those in the past, *Trapeze*, which covers the beginning of Nin's bicoastal life, traveling between her two men, husband Hugh Guiler in New York and lover Rupert Pole in California. There is a reason why volume 5 of *The Diary of Anaïs Nin* is so slim despite covering an eight year period (1947-1955), which is because when it was published both Pole and Guiler were still alive, and Nin could not reveal her secret life for fear of harming them. And the secret life is exactly what *Trapeze* contains. It is an amazing document that chronicles not only the daunting logistics of such a life, but also the toll it took on all three involved—physically, mentally and psychologically. Did Nin really find happiness in this way? Or was it a matter of survival, that no one man or one life could possibly satisfy her needs? The answers are in the book, which will be released as a co-publication between Sky Blue Press and Swallow/Ohio University Press in May of this year. For an excerpt and the introduction to *Trapeze*, refer to volume 13 of this publication.

Also being released this year is *Anaïs Nin: An Unprofessional Study*, an analysis of Nin's work by Kazim Ali. We are happy to provide both an excerpt from and a review of this new title in this issue.

Another monumental addition to the ever-growing list of Nin titles occurred in 2016—the release of *Auletris: Erotica*, which had been unknown to the public (and scholars alike) until a copy surfaced in a university archive. It contains two major erotic stories by Nin, one of which had never been published in any form—in this issue of *A Café in Space* we offer readers a chance to learn the history of *Auletris* and to see an excerpt from the first story. I should add that the book was not published without difficulty. Amazon, the world's largest retailer, made the book unsearchable because, as they stated, it contains "adult content." This banishment drew attention around the world, beginning articles from news.com.au and *The Guardian*, both of whom blasted Amazon for modern-day censorship. The day after the *Guardian* article appeared, Amazon reversed its decision, and *Auletris* is now easily found on its website. I personally want to commend all those on social media and the news agencies who added their voices to the cause, and Amazon for "seeing the light."

Speaking of Nin erotica, the editor of the bestsellers *Delta of Venus* and *Little Birds*, John Ferrone, passed away last spring after a long battle with Parkinson's Disease. His genius, kindness and generosity will be missed. I thank him for his help in the editing of *Mirages: The Unexpurgated Diary of Anaïs Nin* (2013, Sky Blue Press/Swallow Press), the first such diary in seventeen years. His credo was: "Be bold. Do not be afraid to make changes, major changes if necessary. Anaïs deserves the best, and you need to rise to the occasion." Episode 15 of The Anaïs Podcast is dedicated to his memory, as is an article by Tristine Rainer in this issue.

Sky Blue Press is proud to announce that it will be publishing a print version of Britt Arenander's *Anaïs Nin's Lost World: Paris in Words and Pictures 1924-1939*, a look at the Paris Anaïs Nin and Henry Miller once inhabited. Publication is set for the fall of 2017.

We are currently hard at work on the transcription and editing of the next unexpurgated diary, which will cover the years 1955-1966, the era that could be called the "pre-fame years." It begins after Nin's bigamous marriage to Rupert Pole and ends just before the publication of the book that would vault her to fame, *The Diary of Anaïs Nin*, volume one. These were very difficult years for Nin as she struggled to escape obscurity and rejection in the American literary world. It was a time when she, after having several titles published by bona fide publishing houses, resorted to self-publication of *Solar Barque* (1958) and *Cities of the Interior* (1959). It was a time of great frustration and humiliation. But it was also a time when Alan Swallow, Nin's first dedicated American publisher appeared. Around this time Henry Miller reappeared in Nin's life, after his banned books were finally published after the famous obscenity trials of the early 1960s; he was suddenly—and literally—"rich and famous." Miller granted Nin the proceeds of his *Letters to Anaïs Nin* (1965), as a repayment of all the support she had given him during his destitute years. The book not only helped her financially at a time when she desperately needed it, but also put her name in the spotlight as she was preparing to take the great leap of publishing her diary. These years are almost the opposite of the Paris years in the 1930s when it was Nin who fed Miller, encouraged him, inspired him when he was at the threshold of his own first major publication. This volume is tentatively called *The Diary of Others*.

The Anaïs Nin Podcast has had some fabulous guests this past year—Barbara Kraft, whose *Henry Miller: The Last Days* was published by Sky Blue Press; Henry Miller himself, being interviewed by Kraft in 1979; Cindy Shapiro, the force behind the wildly successful *Anaïs: A Dance Opera*; Gayle Nin Rosenkrantz, Anaïs Nin's niece; and a panel discussion about *Auletris* with erotica editor/writer/podcaster Rose Caraway, writer/publisher Lana Fox, women's issues expert Anaín Bjorkquist, and Nin scholar Jessica Gilbey. For a complete list of this year's podcasts, see the index at the end of this issue; for earlier episodes, refer to volume 13 of this publication. ❖

Paul Herron

Introduction to *Auletris: Erotica*

Anaïs Nin is considered by many as the godmother or, as Nin herself put it, the Madame[1] of feminine erotica, and in writing for a collector at a dollar a page she risked arrest, conviction and imprisonment because of the draconian obscenity laws of the 1940s. In spite of the danger and the much-needed income, Nin didn't take her erotic writing seriously—she said that she "was writing to entertain, under pressure from a client" and that she believed her "style was derived from men's work"[2]—but when it was finally published as *Delta of Venus* and *Little Birds* in the 1970s, it became her bestselling work and gave her name a notoriety that has survived for a generation.

After the publication of Nin's erotica, Harcourt editor John Ferrone declared that only unpublishable scraps of the original remained.[3] So how, then, is it possible that a major work of Nin erotica included in this volume has remained unknown to the public and Nin insiders alike for decades?

Auletris was originally typed on latrine rag (onion paper) with four carbons, making a total of five copies, which were bound into books by the Press of the Sunken Eye (Carmel) in 1950. It consists of two stories. One of them is the unedited version of "Marcel" that appears in an abbreviated form in *Delta of Venus*, and the other is "Life in Provincetown," which was unknown to Nin's literary executor, editor and literary agent, all of whom had a deep and vast knowledge of her work. There is no such manuscript in Nin's archives. Here is how, based on the facts we now have, I believe *Auletris* came to be.

It is widely known that Nin began writing erotica in the early 1940s for a collector or "patron" whose agent was a man named Barnett Ruder in New York. According to Nin's diary, Henry Miller met Ruder in 1940 and was offered a job that would pay him "one hundred dollars a month to write one hundred pages or so especially for [Ruder]—mostly on sex."[4] Miller was in serious need of money, so he accepted. He began writing with the understanding that Ruder was sending his work to a collector who financed the operation, although Miller suspected that Ruder himself was the actual collector.[5] The writing soon became drudgery, and Miller felt enslaved. When Doubleday offered him a contract for a "book on America," which eventually became *The Air-Conditioned Nightmare*, Miller dropped the erotic writing altogether.

Nin, who was Miller's longtime lover and *patronne*, agreed to finance Miller's tour of America for the new book. To raise funds, she suggested showing Ruder a revised version of her 1932 diary, which contained the sexually charged passages about the beginning of Nin's relationship with

Miller and his wife June.[6] She also "pasted one of [her] most becoming Louveciennes photographs on the cover."[7] The package was given to Ruder, who said he would see if his patron, an "old millionaire down south," approved. Not surprisingly, he did, and Nin's career of literary prostitution, as she called it, began.

Between 1940 and 1942 Nin produced at least 850 pages of erotica, not including what was written by a group of literary friends she gathered together to increase the page count. Nin, who rarely destroyed any of her writing, kept the carbons for more than thirty years. In the 1970s her Los Angeles lover Rupert Pole felt there was a bestseller wasting away in her archive.[8] Nin, who discounted the erotic writing as imitative of male pornographers, nixed the idea of publishing it, fearing it would damage her standing in literature. But Pole was persistent, and after a long period of cajoling, he persuaded her to let John Ferrone offer a professional opinion.[9]

It was nearly a year later that Ferrone read the story "The Hungarian Adventurer" on a visit to Pole and Nin in Los Angeles. He was convinced that Pole was right about the erotica and that Nin was wrong. Ferrone told Nin that her erotica was not imitative of male writing at all, but uniquely feminine, rich, beautifully written, literary and ground-breaking. Nin agreed to let Harcourt publish the erotica and told Ferrone he could edit it however he thought best.[10] Ferrone took the entire collection with him back to New York and set about the massive task of unraveling the complicated and entangled tales and make them into cohesive stories. Because Nin was seriously ill with cancer by then, Ferrone wasn't able to ask for her opinions or explanations and was completely on his own.

The initial collection, *Delta of Venus*, was published only months after Nin's death in 1977. It became an instant critical and commercial success, remaining on *The New York Times* best-seller list for thirty-six weeks, and, as Ferrone later noted, "[m]ore royalties would pour in from the sales of Delta than from all of [Nin's] previous books put together."[11] *The New York Times Book Review* called *Delta of Venus* "a joyous display of the erotic imagination," and *Cosmopolitan* said it was "inventive, sophisticated" and "highly elegant naughtiness." *Little Birds*, the second volume of Nin erotica, also edited by Ferrone, enjoyed similar success two years later.

Ferrone said that "[s]lightly more than half of the 850 pages ended up in *Delta*, and another thirty percent was used in the second volume, *Little Birds*. The rest, about a hundred pages of fragments and trimmings, was left unpublished."[12] Ferrone had no reason to believe that there was any viable Nin erotica yet to be published. Then, in 1985, he received a letter from a colleague telling him that Harris Auction Galleries in Baltimore had approached Harcourt seeking bibliographic information on Anaïs Nin, which was nothing unusual. But the letter contained a bombshell: Harris claimed it was about to auction off a book called *Auletris* that consisted of two erotic stories written by "A. Nin," and that one of them "might be a discovery."[13] While one of the stories ("Marcel") was familiar to the Harcourt editors, the other, "Life in Provincetown," was unknown to all concerned. Could it be that somehow a major piece of Nin erotica had been lost for four decades and was suddenly found?

The volume of *Auletris* Harris was planning to auction off was copy number three of five. While there is no definitive proof that any copies were sold, a penciled-in price of $35.00 for copy number three indicates it is possible. Copy number one is housed at UCLA, and number four is found in the George Howard Papers at USC. The whereabouts of the remaining copies are unknown.

George Howard was based in Los Angeles in the early 1940s and was befriended by Miller. Miller suggested that Nin send typescripts of the erotica written for Ruder to Howard for possible sale in California.[14] According to the contents list of his archive, Howard had copies of not only the stories in *Auletris*, but much of the erotica included in *Delta of Venus* and *Little Birds*, as well as the stories in Miller's *Opus Pistorum*. According to Miller biographer Robert Ferguson, Howard had offered the stories of *Opus* to a friend of Miller's[15] in 1950. When the friend asked Miller about the stories, Miller denied writing them,[16] though many Miller scholars believe he is indeed the author.

The Miller stories were ostensibly collected in *Opus Pistorum* by Press of the Sunken Eye in 1950, the same year that Howard had tried to sell them to Miller's friend. Press of the Sunken Eye issued *Auletris* during the same year. Since both Miller and Nin had sent Howard copies of their erotica, and we know that Howard was trying to sell Miller's, it is probable that he also tried to sell Nin's and eventually found a buyer for both.

According to Harris Galleries' description of *Auletris*, the man who retyped *Auletris* and *Opus Pistorum* was Milton Luboviski.[17] Both books were produced by Press of the Sunken Eye in 1950, and while they were created with different typewriters, Harris Galleries says that "the format of both works is very similar."[18] Both books were typed with four carbons, adding up to five copies each, including the ribbon copy.

So we have an idea of how "Life in Provincetown" and "Marcel" wound up in Luboviski's hands, but why was "Life in Provincetown" unknown for so long? Was it that the story somehow got lost during the three decades the carbons were in Nin's archive? This seems unlikely because Nin was organized and meticulous when it came to her work—the only major item that she ever lost was a volume of her childhood diary.[19] Perhaps the typescript she sent to Miller was the only one. It could be that she didn't notice this, or perhaps she sent it to Howard with the understanding he would send it back after copying it. There is also a January 10, 1942 letter[20] from Miller to Howard asking about a "missing folder of erotica." Could "Life in Provincetown" have been in that folder?

Since there seems to be no original carbon of "Life in Provincetown" in existence, how can we be certain it is Nin's work? And if it is her work, how do we know that Luboviski or someone else didn't tinker with it?

Nin's prose style is distinct, with unique terminology and phrasing. In other words, her work is easily recognized. "Life in Provincetown" fits in seamlessly with the stories in *Delta of Venus* and *Little Birds*, and there is nothing that would make a seasoned Nin reader suspicious of its authorship. Furthermore, it appears with an erotic story known to be by her, "Marcel." It is unlikely that anyone would use a Nin story with a non-Nin story in the same book. As for Luboviski editing the story, we must consider that he was merely trying to make money off someone else's work. What incentive would there have been to edit or rewrite passages? One indication of editing would have been textual or stylistic alterations to "Marcel," but when compared to the *Delta* version, the only significant changes are extensive cuts by Ferrone. For this reason, it is logical to conclude that "Life in Provincetown" appears as Nin wrote it.

It is obvious that whoever wrote "Life in Provincetown" was familiar with the town and the artists' community within. We know from Nin's diaries that she spent a good deal of time in Provincetown in the 1940s, and she was sexually involved with some people she met there.[21]

The *Auletris* version of "Marcel" is 51 pages long, as opposed to the 17 pages in *Delta of Venus*. John Ferrone said that there were two major reasons for heavy edits in the erotica—one was that "many [stories] had to be carved out of long, episodic narratives that contained tales within tales. They needed beginnings and endings, and often titles as well."[22] The other was censorship. Ferrone says that "[i]t was clear from the beginning that Anaïs, never dreaming of publication, had drawn on the outlines of her own life for inspiration, as well as on the Kama Sutra and Krafft-Ebing. It would have been easy for readers to mistake fiction for autobiography. There were many other autobiographical parallels, some probably close to fact. It becomes evident [...] that Anaïs borrowed heavily from her journal material, as she did for all of her fiction."[23] Because some of the characters were based on people still living, Ferrone felt the need to either render them unrecognizable or to excise them altogether. Today, no such restrictions exist.

Why didn't Harcourt, or anyone else, publish *Auletris*? It's easy to see why no one in 1986 would republish any version of "Marcel," the heavily edited version of which was already included in *Delta of Venus*. And perhaps because of the odd length of "Life in Provincetown" (43 typewritten pages), it wouldn't make sense for a commercial publisher to release it on its own.

This edition of *Auletris* is reproduced as it appears in the original, minus misspellings, typos and minor formatting problems, allowing the reader to see Nin's words as they were intended for the collector, as well as providing an opportunity to see how John Ferrone went about creating a bestseller from the raw material. ❖

Works cited

Dearborn, Mary. *The Happiest Man Alive: A Biography of Henry Miller*. New York: Simon & Schuster, 1991.

Ferguson, Robert. *Henry Miller: A Life*. New York: W. W. Norton, 1991.

Ferrone, John. "The Making of *Delta of Venus*," *A Café in Space: The Anaïs Nin Literary Journal*, volume 7. Santa Fe, NM: Sky Blue Press, 2010.

Nin, Anaïs. *The Diary of Anaïs Nin 1939-1943* (volume 3). New York: Harcourt Brace Jovanovich, 1969.

----. *Linotte: The Early Diary of Anaïs Nin, 1914-1920*. New York: Harcourt Brace Jovanovich, 1978.

----. *Mirages: The Unexpurgated Diary of Anaïs Nin, 1939-1947*. Athens, OH: Swallow Press/ Sky Blue Press, 2013.

Notes

1 On November 4, 1941, Nin writes: "I gather the poets around me, and persuade them to write erotica, communicating eroticism and spreading this writing that is usually suppressed, giving them both the poison of disintegration and perhaps a way of purification, for all of us have violent explosions of poetry, and we eject the purely sexual as fervently as if we had taken vows of chastity. A purge, and not debauchery, results from the infiltration of erotic confessions. [Harvey] Breit, [George] Barker, Robert [Duncan]. A house of prostitution. I, the Madame, supplying the Old Man with moments of perverse felicity, his drug..." (*Mirages*, p. 81)

2 Postscript to the Introduction of *Delta of Venus*, p. xvi.

3 Ferrone, p. 56.

4 *Mirages*, p. 42.

5 *Diary 3*, pp. 56-57.

6 *Mirages*, p. 41. Nin writes: "I could give [Ruder] copies of the diary in exchange for money for Henry's trip. Virginia [Admiral] copied diary 32, I revised it, changed the names..."

7 *Mirages*, p. 42.

8 Ferrone, p. 53.

9 Ferrone, p. 54.

10 Ferrone, p. 55.

11 Ferrone, p. 59.

12 Ferrone, p. 56.

13 In a letter to Rupert Pole dated January 16, 1986, Ferrone says that Harris Galleries had "two of Anaïs's erotica manuscripts, bound. One is called 'Marcel,' and was published in *Delta*. The other is called 'Life in Provincetown' and appears to not have been published."

[14] In Box 1, Folder 2 of the Howard archive, a letter dated March 26, 1941 and signed by Anaïs Nin asks Howard if he wishes to see more pages of the manuscripts from which Miller had previously given him a sample. She also entreats him to suggest a way of disposing of the manuscript in order to finance Miller's tour of America.

In Box 1, Folder 3, there is a letter dated October 11, 1941 and signed by Henry Miller in which he says that he is sending Howard a typescript of pornographic material done by Nin and informing Howard of an abridged version of the Diary, which covers 1930-1935 in Paris.

[15] Ferguson cites a letter from Miller's friend Rives Childs in which he tells Miller the names of the stories Howard offered him. Miller flatly denied writing the stories. (*Henry Miller: A Life*, pp. 277-278.)

[16] Ferguson posits that Miller may have been "ashamed" of his role in pornography (p. 277). Another Miller biographer, Mary Dearborn, thinks that Miller was continuing to "distance himself from Nin in deference to her wishes that their relationship remain secret" (p. 211). Neither biographer questions Miller's authorship of *Opus Pistorum*.

[17] Milton Luboviski, in his "Epilogue" of the 1983 Grove Press edition of *Opus Pistorum*, claimed that Miller wrote for him in the early 1940s, which counters Ferguson's (and Nin's) account that he wrote the original material for Ruder.

[18] From a rough draft of the description of *Auletris*, Harris Galleries, 1986.

[19] "A manuscript of the diary covering the period from January 1918 to March 1919 was lost." *Linotte*, p. 207.

[20] The letter is in Box 1, Folder 7 of the George Howard papers.

[21] See pp. 58-85 in *Mirages*.

[22] The *Auletris* version of "Marcel" contains fragments of other stories that appear in *Delta of Venus*, including "Mathilde," "Mandra" and "Miriam."

[23] Ferrone, p. 56

Anaïs Nin

"Life in Provincetown"

An excerpt from Auletris: Erotica

One long main street running along the Bay outline, Portuguese fishermen sitting in circles like the Italians and chatting. Behind the houses on the main street are wharves which project out on the water at various lengths. On these wharves are the huts, shacks, which the fishermen once used to store their nets, tools, and the boats to be repaired. It is here that the artists live. The roofs are peaked and beamed. Everything is made of rough wood like the inside of some old ship. At high tide the water runs under the wharves, at low tide it exposes a long stretch of sand.

The walls are thin. One can hear everything. Often the shades are not down, and one can see everything.

There are no guardians, no one to say: stop the noise, or to see at what time one comes home. No superintendents, house owners. Just the lonely wharves, in darkness at night, the sound of the water, and little crooked shack-like studios occupied by a variety of people.

The town is full of soldiers, sailors, and beautiful Portuguese girls...and summer visitors in shorts.

There is one movie, one bar where women are not admitted and several night clubs.

In one studio there lived one of the artist's models, whose mouth was so big, so full, so prominent, that one could see nothing else. When she looked at one, one could notice only the mouth, like the mouth of a negress. She rouged too heavily, and then powdered her face white, so that the mouth stood out even more and was able to eclipse the rest of the face and even the body.

As one knew she was a model, well known in the Village in New York, one assumed she had a beautiful body, but somehow one only looked at the mouth. Somehow or other one imagined the other mouth to be equally luxuriant, equally prominent. Just as one felt that the thin-lipped mouths of Puritan women must he the exact replicas of their thin-lipped sexuality.

This mouth wore a flaming red bathing suit from morning till evening. She lived alone with the shades always up. One could watch her dress in the morning. One could see her asleep, first of all, late in the morning, sprawled on her bed in great disorder. That was when she was alone. She was rarely alone. Very often she lay in bed completely concealed by some heavy arm, or a man's body...

They slept as if they had had a bout and were exhausted. Slept on through the morning, in each other's arms. Locked as they were, it was difficult to imagine that this locked embrace was only temporary. The next evening it would be a different man. The model had such a simple way of solving her problem. When she saw a handsome man in the street, she slipped her arm through his, looked up at his face, smiling, and said, "Hello."

It was as simple as that. Rarely was she given a cold hello because of her mouth.

Unlocking herself from the embrace of her night visitor she would rush to her work as a model, so everyone in Provincetown knew her body more or less intimately. The painting classes knew it from long hours of contemplation, and the rest of the town, from such bouts as I have mentioned.

The only one she could not lure so easily to her room was her very own neighbor, the handsomest boy in all the town, the son of a Portuguese fisherman, now captain of a sailing yacht which took visitors around the Cape at night for one dollar.

He slept next door to her. Before he had seen her he had heard all the tumult in her room; the night before, he had heard a particular grunt of satisfaction from some heavy body, and then a woman's delighted laughter, such a laughter as he had never heard.

To begin with he had never heard of a woman laughing while love-making. They always grew so serious and intense, the gayest of them. He had known plenty in his sailor life. They always grew serious. Never even smiled, as if love-making, even with a stranger, were an intense affair, not to be treated lightly.

Their pleasure was always like the pleasure of an animal, dark rather, with strange sounds. Animals do not laugh. Women became animals at night, surely, as these legends told us. More so even than men.

But not the richly-mouthed model. She laughed like a negress being tickled. Every caress made her laugh obscenely. And there was a different kind of laughter for each part of the body. Lying in the dark, on the other side of the wall, he could almost divine where she was being touched.

At first it was her feet, surely, and it tickled her because she giggled. It must have been only the external portions of her body, for she laughed gaily, lightly. The man with her must have been touching her ribs, her shoulders, her arms, her legs. Suddenly, her laughter changed. It was modulated as if she were being slightly hurt, and it was that she was growing vulnerable.

He could tell. She laughed like someone plunging into too cold water, and gasping, and then feeling the warm reaction, and enjoying the new sensation.

She laughed as if pleasure were new and beginning to invade her. Ah..... ahh.....came her voice in the darkness. If he could have seen her move he would not have been as clearly aware of her pleasure. He felt this pleasure of hers rippling through his muscles. The walls were so thin he could feel it all in his body. Ah.....ahh.....there was a silence. This silence disturbed the Portuguese more than anything. What could keep her so still, after her rippling and open pleasure? What caress could silence her suddenly as if too profound to cause an exterior proof of joy? He tried to divine. He knew she was naked, for he had heard her say, "Let's take all our clothes off." What was the man doing to her? No sound. The Portuguese felt ripples covering his strong, dark body. He felt close to a mystery. He expected her to cry out any moment from uncontainable ecstasy. Instead there came out of the darkness, a long, prolonged low laughter, guttural, rich, low, obscene...

The other mouth—surely the man had opened his way into the other mouth, the luxuriant, thick, rich sexual mouth she carried almost exposed for everyone to see in her twin mouth of her face...for everyone to see the thickness and fullness of her sexual feelings...ripe and open and red... Ah..... Ah.....came the voice. The flesh indented by the attack of the man, yielding, and with guttural cries that revealed the thrusts made into it, each thrust accompanied by a long ahhhhhh.....ahhhhhhh of pleasure, until her voice sank.

And then again a silence. And then the voice came as if she were suddenly violently wounded. Ahhh........ The Portuguese's body was burning, tortured with desire. Each cry of the woman raised his penis in the dark. And how it burned. All the wind and sun that had beaten against it, the cold and heat, the salt water, contributed to making it firm and salty and vigorous, and now it stood raised in the dark, leaping at each modulation of the woman's voice. When her last cry came, he almost thought he would come too, so feverish and taut he was, listening to this scene and imagining all its developments...

Silence now. They must have fallen asleep. The Portuguese could not sleep. He rose and slipped on his trousers. He opened the screen door of his studio. There was a light next door. The shades were raised. And there she lay, naked and asleep, with the man fallen over her. No matter how much he desired her, and now it was every moment of the day and night, when he saw her walking about, so naked in her bathing suit that he could see the curled pubic hairs protruding on each side of her tight panties, so naked that the straps often fell from her shoulders and revealed half of her breasts...yet he could not bring himself to become one of those anonymous men who could all give her pleasure.

He could not bring himself to take this body which belonged to everyone and could enjoy anyone's caresses equally. That held him back.

And what difficulty he had in being reserved with her and yet having to listen almost every night to the same scene.

She was indefatigable... "She's a nymphomaniac," he thought. "She never has enough...she is a monster... I don't want to love a monster like that. She is just like her mouth, big and voracious and always hungry. I could never keep her to myself..."

That is not what she thought. She felt somehow, that right next door to her lived the most vigorous of them all. She sensed his vigor. She could not break down his resistance. And then with a feminine clairvoyance she divined what kept him away from her. She decided to sacrifice to him the days of her pleasure. She felt sure or her plan.

Suddenly no one came to see her. Every night he listened and there was no sound of love-making. She lay in her bed, and he could hear her turning over. He could hear the hair pins dropping on the floor when she loosened her hair. But no love-making. He was intrigued. He began to think more and more about her.

One night he heard her sigh. He was unable to sleep. He raised his voice a little and said: "Why are you sighing?"

"I'm here alone and I am remembering a terrible story l heard today. I met a woman on the beach who talked to me. She was a curious, handsome woman, highly strung. Her hands trembled all the time. We started talking. She described her son to me. When he was thirteen he was a beautiful boy with long eyelashes like a girl, a slender body, a fine crop of curly brown hair. He was clever and brilliant.

"They lived in Paris. The boy was abnormally fond of reading. Especially the poets. At thirteen he had already tried smoking and drinking...even drugs. But his mother knew nothing of this. One day alone in the attic apartment they occupied together, while the mother was out, (and she used to stay out all night drinking), he was playing at hanging himself. He had just read the life of a poet who hanged himself in a garret.

"The boy passed the heavy cord around one of the beams and stood on a box and knotted the cord around his neck. He liked to imagine the idea of dying and of being deeply regretted. He liked to picture how his mother would feel, whereas now he was faced every day with a kind of abandonment.

"Well, he tightened the rope around his neck, just playing, and then what he felt at that moment was so amazing: he felt pleasure, a pleasure that went through his body, a sensation he had never known, which started where he urinated, and then spread all over his body. It lasted only while the rope was tight around his neck.

"This discovery amazed and frightened him. He let go of the rope and went back to his books, flushed and disturbed. He could not quite believe it. Strange that where his limp little sex had been before there were great disturbances as if it were filled with a new impetus, and that was not to urinate. A kind of sap was rising and lifting it and hardening it, just at the moment when the cord had tightened around his neck.

"The boy told nobody about this. He wanted to make sure it was real. He spent a restless night thinking he had dreamt it and that the next day he would not experience the same pleasure.

"He patiently waited until the next evening when his mother was out again, and then he climbed on his soap box and placed the noose around his slender neck and pulled slightly.

"The sensation returned. When the cord was tight something delicious and exalting happened in the region of his sex, something never felt before and which was a greater pleasure than that of drinking. He enjoyed this for a few minutes and then stopped because the blood was rushing to his head and his neck was hurting.

"But for several nights he experienced this, waiting always to make sure it was real, and that it depended on the rope. He tried to make it last. He stood there and pulled his head downward, the rope tightening, and watched his own body in its ecstasy of erection. His face grew congested, but the pain around his neck he did not mind.

"The pleasure began always slowly, like wine drinking, a warmth, then a fluid would rush to the sex and fill it like a precious liqueur, and the tautness was exciting and filled him with the desire, vague and mysterious, which he could not fulfill. All of this was a mysterious thing to him. He was afraid to tell his mother and even his comrades. He felt he had made a discovery. The pleasure was so tremendous he was almost jealous of sharing it. He felt obscurely that he would be severely scolded, more than for smoking or drinking. The tension brought about was so great that it exasperated him at times. There was something he could not discover, and that was how to release the tension of this taut joy that almost broke him when it came.

"One night with his head in the tight rope, he let his pleasure invade him slowly. It started in the middle of his body. It flowed all through him, making the body rigid, and burning, filling his little sex with something more potent than liquor, something that ached to be pushed out. That was what he felt, the desire to push it out into space. Perhaps if he tightened the rope a little more... He held his head down to watch his body. The acuteness of the pleasure forced him into a contortion which resembled the contortion of an ejaculation. He pushed his body forward, slipped off the box, and fell into space. As he fell what he had desired happened. But he was not alive to experience it."

"What a terrible story," said the Portuguese. "No wonder you can't sleep."

"There are times when one feels pleasure like this, with almost a desire to put an end to it, it is so strong."

"Would you like me to come over and we'll light the light and talk until you get over your evil impressions?"

"Yes, do come…" said the model.

The Portuguese entered her studio, looking very tall and very dark, filling the room with his vivid and potent presence. The woman's mouth could be seen in the darkness. He lit a candle, and in its flickering light she smiled at him...it was all he could do not to throw himself upon her. Her mouth was so inviting, so swollen...as if for kissing.

He sat near her bed and they talked. But as they talked she fell asleep, and the Portuguese was able to look at her. Her dark hair was all over the pillow, a dark pillow, all around her. Even in the candlelight her mouth shone red, and it was half open like a flame.

The Portuguese approached her and gave her a kiss. She awakened and put her arms around him. He kissed her again. The mouth melted under his strong lips. It was warm and soft and cushioned, as no mouth he had ever tasted.

It yielded to his kiss, opened, and the tips of two tongues met. Her breasts were so hard he felt them against his chest as he kissed her.

What he felt was that he wanted to do something to her that no other man had done—he did not want her to laugh as she had laughed for the others—he wanted to experience something new, and he did not know what it would be.

The minute she laughed she would be the woman all men could possess, and he did not want this. He continued to kiss her and think about it. Something she had not felt yet, laughed at, with pleasure. What new pleasure could he give her?

The story of the boy haunted him. He wanted to frighten her. Above all he wanted her not to laugh, as she had laughed for the other men. The way she abandoned her mouth made him hate her...the way she closed her eyes. She closed her eyes and opened her mouth as if any man, any mouth or penis could please her at the moment.

She was in a trance. Soon she would begin to laugh hoarsely and suggestively if he touched her. First he gripped her backside fiercely with his two hands and brought her up against him, and she felt his virility. It was of such strength and power that she felt it first against her hair, before it penetrated her; she gasped at the electric touch of it.

He buried his mouth deeper into hers, feeling every nook under her lips, under her tongue, feeling her tongue licking at him, flung back at his tongue each time, like a palpitation and vibration between them.

He did not caress her. He pushed himself straight inside of her, firmly, powerfully and then lay still. She had never been so well filled, every nook of her flesh filled by this strong virility, and it seemed to her that once inside of her it stretched a little more, pushed the walls of her soft flesh, installed itself leisurely, for good.

That was what she loved, the way he nestled inside of her, so completely as if to stay. She could enjoy him leisurely too. She loved this. The feel of the hard sex inside of her, not moving, nestled there, and only vibrating when she contracted to feel it more. Imperceptibly at times he withdrew, just slightly, as if to make room for the contractions which pressed him, and lured him back into the depths of her.

She did not laugh. She was strangely silent. The quietness with which he entered her, without caresses, and the quietness with which he lay inside her, as if to feel every motion and ripple of her flash around his sex. The quietness and hardness of his penis filling her completely, so that when the womb began to breathe, as it were, inhaling and exhaling there in the dark, to envelop him, encompass him and then open like a mouth and close again, she felt a quiet, long, drawn-out pleasure, which made her silent.

He was enjoying reaching into the depths of her and not moving, not giving her an active pleasure. They lay entangled, his naked body the whole length of her, and she flung back, legs apart, and eyes closed, and their mouths together.

Then the pleasure was too much for her; she wanted to move, to push against him, to feel him deeper, to cling and rub against him, but he prevented her from doing so, with such a strength of his powerful sailor muscles that she was paralyzed. Without moving inside of her, his bigness, and hardness, stirred her. She continued to lick and press and caress him with her womb, trying to engulf him more, trying to move more inside of herself since he didn't let her move her body.

Her body he kept pinned and paralyzed. Then as she contracted and moved she felt her pleasure increasing, and she was nearing her paroxysm, and out of her closed mouth there struggled to escape some guttural sound, from the depths of her belly, that would have been laughter of pleasure if he had permitted it, but he suddenly flung his two hands around her neck and whispered fiercely: "If you laugh I will strangle you!"

A strange fear came into her eyes; the sounds of pleasure died suddenly, but she could not stop the mounting, invading pleasure like some molten magical lava beginning to pour through her veins, inflaming her flesh, and he kept his hands around her throat, and she thought that her pleasure was all that mattered; she felt suddenly like the boy that she must have her ultimate pleasure for she could not control it, the violence with which it ran through her veins and sought to explode in her.

In her fear, she was immobilized, yet she continued to contract in her womb and he felt this, and it gave her pleasure to see that pleasure was getting hold of his body too, and that he might be forced to release his grip on her throat, but he did not release it—he tightened it—and she experienced a real and absolute fear then, that in his pleasure he might strangle her, for his pleasure was mixed with hatred, hatred to think she could so easily be made to feel this joy, responding to it like a perfect animal, not to him alone, but to all...to any man with a mouth to kiss, and an erect penis...

In spite of the fear, and with the fear there came a surcharged, tense joy in her, running through all her veins, tickling the soles of her feet, running up along the inside of her legs, touching off the backside and warming it, touching the tips of the breasts as if he were caressing her, nothing but this wine of desire coursing now all inside of her, and the pain of his hands on her neck could not stop it—it increased.

If she had laughed obscenely with her pleasure he would have tightened his hands, perhaps strangled her. But instead of laughing, as her pleasure was so excruciating, and as he did not move and therefore did not bring it to an end, but prolonged the excruciating suspense, a strange long whining sound came from her as if she were in pain, a deep animal whine which he loved and which then threw him with new fervor on her and loosened his hands, and then he moved, he moved in all directions, like a tourniquet, round and round, not stopping, as if he would plough her completely and absolutely, leaving no corner untouched, and she moaned, she did not laugh, she moaned in the grip of such a deep joy that she wept... ❖

Erotic card used for the cover of *Auletris*

The cover of *Auletris* has its own story. Among some items found in Anaïs Nin's Los Angeles studio was a very old erotic drawing on a card with a thumbtack hole in it. In Nin's 1920s diary, she mentions that she and her husband Hugh Guiler rented an apartment with many "erotic photographs" tacked to the walls. While there is no way to verify that the card found in the studio is one of them, at least there is a chance it could be.

When the cover was finished, it received rave reviews from those who saw it, with one notable exception—Amazon, who felt that the two dots representing nipples was "adult content." This, and the fact the book is indeed erotica, was reason enough for Amazon to banish *Auletris* to its "adult content dungeon," where books face invisibility and non-existent sales. After a media blitz, Amazon finally released the book to the general public.

Kazim Ali

Painting

An excerpt from Anaïs Nin: An Unprofessional Study

Of all the arts, Nin's metaphors and images depend most upon the plastic and visual and her work is haunted by painting and painters, both characters and actual artists. Jay. Hans. Renate. Jean Varda. Paul Klee. Marcel Duchamp.

Though light shimmers and moves on Stella's screen, the life that unfolds there is life at a distance. Nin saw always the transformative possibilities of the plastic arts of painting and collage and sculpture and her work is saturated with this visual experience.

Art and the making of art is always developed as a metaphor for personal freedom. In *Children of the Albatross*, the young men who come to Djuna's apartment feel that it is a free and creative space. Paul makes a little bird to hang from Djuna's ceiling while Lawrence dyes the hamster's hair blue.

Similarly destruction of art is the purest of brutalities: in a famous scene from *Four-Chambered Heart*, Rango asks Djuna to burn her books because they represent her life separate from him. Even more brutally, because Djuna reasons the books "had not prepared her for moments such as this," she complies. "All these novels so carefully concealing the truth about character, about the obscurities, the tangles, the mysteries," Djuna rails, "Words words words words and no revelation of the pitfalls, the abysms in which human beings found themselves. Let him burn them all; they deserved their fate" (*Cities of the Interior*, p. 272).

In her 1946 manifesto "Realism and Reality," Nin writes, "The best way to approach my [writing] is as one regards modern painting. I intend the greater part of my writing to be received directly through the senses, as one receives painting and music…a column can signify more than a whole house…[Brancusi] achieved the closest expression of the flight of a bird by eliminating the wings" (*Mystic of Sex*, p. 23).

Critic Lloyd Morris elaborates a little further in saying that Nin "is not, in the usual sense, trying to tell a story. Her object is to reveal experience directly. She wishes to immerse readers in that flow sensibility and reflection from which human beings distill the significance of what they do and suffer" (qtd. Hinz, p. 52).

Both Sabina and Djuna think of themselves as the woman depicted in Duchamp's painting "Nude Descending a Staircase."

For Djuna, this moment comes just after she and Rango experience their conflict over the usefulness of political involvement over art. Rango has just met Djuna's friend Sabina and doesn't like her. Djuna feels like "not one but many Djunas," like "multiple selves grown in various proportions, not singly…not moving in one direction, but composed of multiple juxtapositions revealing endless spirals of character as the earth revealed its strata, an infinite feeling of constellations expanding…" (*Cities*, p. 343).

Djuna could be describing Nin's entire project in *Cities of the Interior*, her theory of character in those novels and in her fiction, in general.

Not just "Djuna, meet Djuna" but also "Djuna meet Sabina." Evans is right then: the application of the meditation on the painting *does* cause the characters to "blur and overlap in the reader's mind."

Which seems Nin's intent, it now seems almost too obvious to say.

When Sabina at the close of *Spy* is walking home, despondently, feeling like she can't just return to Alan one more time, she thinks of the Duchamp painting, feeling like "eight or ten outlines of the same women, like many multiple exposures of a woman's personality…walking down the stairs in unison." If she went home now, she thinks, "it would be like detaching one of these cut-outs of a woman…a divided woman" (*Cities*, p. 453).

She understands her own need for other lovers as stemming from this feeling of fragmentation: "Each year, just as a tree puts forth a new ring of growth, she should have been able to say: 'Alan, here is a new version of Sabina. Add it to the rest, fuse them well, hold them all at once…or else divided, separated, each image will live a life of its own…"

The stimulus for Djuna retreating into her "cities of the interior" at the café table at the conclusion of *Children of the Albatross*—Michael's question "Has Paul gone to India yet?"—manifests in the sudden grinding to a halt of the organ music, but is described visually through the monkey's red Turkish cap dropping streetward.

For a surreal and non-narrative fiction, *House of Incest* is soaked in the visual—fish of velvet, lace and organdy, grilled mosque windows, each room of Jeanne's house painted a different color, even the chapter headings each have an alchemical symbol. It seems only a short leap from to make a film of excerpts from the book, but the real visual synthesis happens when Nin adds a set of photomontages created by Val Telberg to future printings.

"I looked upon a clock to find the truth," she writes of time, the ultimate abstraction, yet what follows is told in visual metaphor: "The hours were passing like ivory chess figures, striking piano notes, and the minutes raced on wires like tin soldiers" (*House of Incest*, p. 41).

Throughout the novels, visual expressions help to see the subliminal reality: the two pianos in the rain. The mirrors in the garden. The oft-repeated synesthetic line, "the street organ was unwinding *Carmen* from its roll of tinfoil voices." A woman lying on the beach with her eyes closed. A doll floating in the river after the flood, its china face washed clean of its features.

Jay tells a story of his friend, a painter. Peter lived in a bare studio apartment. He tricks the concierge into thinking he is going to win a rich painting prize. She agrees to let the rent slide. While he paints, she camps out in the courtyard. They are great friends while he paints, but when the paper prints the name of the actual winner of the prize, she flies into a rage. Storming his apartment she sees in horror a body hanging from the ceiling. But what the police cut down is a mannequin of wax, dressed in rags, carefully painted to look like Peter. "After that," says Jay, "his luck turned...he seemed to have killed the self who had been a failure." The reader is fool because ordinarily the point of Jay's rambling stories are the comic narrative themselves, but here—as in the much later novel *Collages*—the real point in the moment of self-transformation enacted by the painter's own act of creativity.

Nin's humor was always of the black variety. The artist is a trickster, not really a cad, but always, like Woolf's villager-actors in *Between the Acts*, holding up mirrors in the garden.

She completes her "continuous novel" in 1959 (though two years later she would feel inspired to add the coda to the final novel) and in the California sunshine, with a whole group of new friends, she returns to her two earliest fictive forms—the more symbolic narrative of *House of Incest* and the short fiction form of *Under a Glass Bell*—to write her last piece of fiction, *Collages*, which she publishes in 1964 and which critic Philip K. Jason calls her "swan song to fiction" (Jason, p. 70).

It is the novel that will give her the technical tools once and for all to begin revising the *Diary* for publication, which she will begin doing immediately upon completion and spend the nine following years editing six volumes of *Diary* (the seventh will be completed by Rupert Pole after her death).

Most Nin critics have placed their greatest emphasis on look at ways that the *Diary* was the laboratory or genesis for the fiction, but we can also understand that the reverse is also true.

Collages is a novel that uses as its structural conceit the visual art of Jean Varda.

Duchamp's painting expressed a neurosis of the fragmented self, but Varda's collage "Women Reconstructing the World" gives Nin a positive model of how the fragment or the shard can be used in service of re-integration.

Rather than concerning itself with a single, main personage, it is the ensemble of sometimes unrelated characters that drives the dramatic action of *Collages*. If *A Spy in the House of Love* is destined for the big screen, then *Collages* would make a wonderful and witty short television series.

Though more experimental in its episodic and non-Aristotelian structure and ambition, *Collages* actually retains a much more mainstream discursive, linear, narrative style than Nin's earlier novels which, while fragmented in terms of plot very much retained a dramatic structure centered around the development and growth of individual characters.

Ladders to Fire built on and obsessed on a smaller focus of characters, though has moments of digression, for example the sections about Helen. *Children of the Albatross* comes closest to a similar structure as *Collages*—episodes loosely grouped into three acts, though *Collages* does not retained the heightened, ritualistic choreographic feeling of that earlier novel; it fees much more natural and spontaneous as it unfolds. *Four-Chambered Heart, A Spy in the House of Love* and *Solar Barque* as we already discussed, each fixate on the experiences of a single character, and everyone else revolves around her. In a way *Collages* is almost a riposte to the later novels of *Cities of the Interior*—it introduces a main character, Renate, then allows her to be the eye around which the hurricane of everyone else's drama turns.

The coda section added to *Solar Barque* of course disrupts the unity of that book and links it to the larger continuous whole of *Cities of the Interior*. In a way, it is that coda—the recounting of Lillian's journey to wholeness reflecting on her relationships with Jay, Sabina and Djuna—that sets up and makes possible a heroine like Renate.

In the first two episodes, Nin begins telling the story of Renate, a woman who grows up in Vienna, and leaves for Mexico, where she frequents The Black Pearl, the same nightclub Lillian once played at, thus linking the two characters by locale.

In the third vignette, Renate moves to California after a disastrous relationship with Bruce in Mexico. Bruce returns to her and begs for another chance, giving her the gift of many puzzle boxes. Whenever she feels she does not understand him, she is to open a puzzle box and inside will find a story of his past. At first the reader is excited, seeing in this gesture perhaps an analog for Nin and her diary and believing the relationship might be saved. Then a more dramatic and perhaps more truthful thing happens: she reads one of them and decides she cannot face all of his secrets and so burns the boxes.

This destruction of art is not the same as Rango's burning of Djuna's books. It is rather Renate's reaction to reading the story—she is preserving their present relationship by refusing the "conclusion" the texts in the boxes would provide.

As the French consul's wife is later told, "Nothing is ever finished."

Continuing the cleansing by fire, in the next scene Renate visits the Laundromat with all of the sheets and linens of the house "stained with the marks of love" and hears the story of the man who works there, who followed his wife from their native Hungary to California. Bruce disappears from the narrative here and the reader might well assume the relationship is over though one has not been told such.

Always in an episodic narrative what is skipped over is at least as interesting as what is left.

As if the mention of the larger world by the launderer had spurred an interest in landscape, the next vignette tells of the small towns of California spread into the hills away from Malibu. A painter drives out to set up shop and paint inhabitants and sell the paintings. We are not told the painter is Renate in disguise until halfway through the chapter. The story of Raven is narrated in which her pet raven assumes her weaknesses while she takes the bird's strengths.

In the seventh episode, Renate drives the coastal highway and hears another story of transformation—a man who dreams himself turning into a seal. These stories all reinforce the notion of transmutation, and a transmutation by creative practice. Because Renate has spoken of the Black Pearl, Lillian Beye is on the reader's mind and the code of *Seduction of the Minotaur* assumes somewhat of a different valence—in retrospect Lillian has indeed effected a transformation by her performance of jazz music in the alchemically-inflected Golconda.

Collages also has three rough acts—these first seven episodes which recount Renate's childhood and Europe and then moving and settling in California comprise the first such act. What follows are nine more episodes; rather than organized around a character—Renate—these are spatially unified by their setting—the Paradise Inn, a restaurant and nightclub where Renate works as a hostess. Many characters including Varda, Leontine the Haitian dancer, Henri the French chef, Nina the actress, Nobuko, Colonel Tishnar and of course the French Consul's wife, (based on the British historian Lesley Branch) the beautiful and talented woman who captures Renate's imagination and whose story gives the novel its dramatic and poetic center of gravity. Was Marguerite Duras aware of *Collages* when she wrote and published *The Vice Consul* the following year?

If Lillian, at the completion of *Seduction of the Minotaur* seems headed home with some sense of wholeness (if not closure), then *Collages* can be seen as the psychic sequel to that book. Unlike Lillian, Renate, who also frequents the Black Pearl when she is in Mexico, decides not to return to Europe. Even after meeting a neurotic and fussy American (whom she seems not to judge at all—a stark contrast from Lillian, Djuna and Sabina all, who are quick to analyze both themselves and others), Renate decides that California is the life for her.

The opening act of *Collages* recounts her transformation. Whereas the other novels end either at the point of frustration or inability to transform (*Ladders to Fire*, *Children of the Albatross*), or at the instant itself of transformation (*Four-Chambered Heart*, *A Spy in the House of Love*, the original *Solar Barque*), only *Collages* takes as its germinal opening gesture the story of transformation itself—from the stone statues of Vienna, unable to ever change, to the quick changing figures of California, including the Seal-Man and Raven.

Lillian is not the only character from the earlier novels that Renate seems to embody. As a painter one can link her Jay; in fact, she repeats Jay's earlier behavior of locking up her lover and leaving the room. When Bruce, like Lillian in the earlier novel, takes umbrage at being locked in the room, Renate laughs and explains as Djuna earlier explained to Lillian, that perhaps it was her secret desire to keep Bruce to herself that made her lock him in the room.

The second act of *Collages* introduces the group of people around Renate, illuminating parts of character by creating a more composite-like picture, similar to the narrative strategy employed by Woolf in *Jacob's Room*, or Duras in *The Vice Consul.*

After three episodes telling the stories of Henri, Leontine and Varda, Renate again appears on the scene in a very brief episode in which Varda, the collage artist, admires the lining of her fabulous coat. Without hesitation Renate takes a pair of large scissors and cuts him a large piece of fabric from the coat to use as collage material. It's an act of generosity of course from one artist—Nin—to another—Varda, the man not the character.

And then suddenly, in the thirteenth episode of the book, unseen since episode four, Bruce is once again with Renate at the Paradise Inn. As in the scattered episodes of *Spy* this helps to build in a certain sense of timelessness or spatial arrangement to episodes of *Collages*. One is hard pressed to read the linearity of the episodes and in a sense this introduces into the text a resistance to being read as a typical narrative novel and reintroduces the concept of seeing the parts simultaneously; rather than passively being *told* a story, the reader must actively experience the episodes "through the senses" as in modern painting, the way Nin intended. Rather than a chain of events, it is a composite series meant to be seen and experienced at once.

Nina the failed actress, Nobuko the aspiring actress, the Consul's wife, and the failed romance of Tessa and the Colonel are then told in a second series of brief episodes, before the "second act" of *Collages* closes with a story of Renate's failure to create a magazine; dreams to create art cannot always compete with material realities.

Hope and potential govern the opening movements of *Collages* and frustration of potential and failure of love govern the second half, though Nobuko, Varda and Leontine each offer a portrait of what might happen if the artist herself internalizes the detritus or ruin—in Varda's case to literally make art out of that ruin, the scraps left behind.

In the final three episodes the scene shifts abruptly to New York, where Renate has gone for an exhibit of her paintings. Two jarring things happen in the closing pages of *Collages*. First, the sunny and hopeful western landscape is replaced by the gritty and harsh New York. This atmospheric shift is made doubly harsh by the recounting of the story of Lisa, a once successful artist in Mexico who has allowed herself to be imprisoned in a terrible marriage with a man who doesn't understand her, a man who "awakened her from her dream of Acapulco with a cigar flavored kiss from the ashcan painting period of her childhood."

And secondly, after providing the McGuffin for the closing episode taking place in New York—an exhibit of her paintings—Renate more or less disappears as a protagonist from the book. As the closing of *Ladders to Fire* was taken away from Lillian and given to Sabina and Djuna, as the narrator of *House of Incest* becomes a spectator in the closing scene of that book, so too is the closing of *Collages* given to the new character of Doctor Mann, who has come to New York from Israel to search for the elusive writer Judith Sands.

Dr. Mann feels that he is the character in Sands' book and is obsessed with meeting her face to face. But before you read these episodes as weird non-sequitur consider that Dr. Mann himself is another facet of Renate. Nin met the painter Renate Druks in California and used her portrait, along with those of Varda, of Josephine Premice (the basis for Leontine), and of others she knew like Lesley Branch, as materials in constructing this novel, just like one of Varda's collages.

Rather than doing the deep internal analysis that Nin's earlier characters do, these characters seem content with telling their own stories and allowing the reader to construct meaning on her own.

And so the drama of Doctor Mann (who sees in himself as a character from Judith Sands' novel, a character that seems to resemble Matthew O'Connor from Djuna Barnes' book *Nightwood*) and Judith Sands (a caricature-portrait of the elusive Barnes) can be read also as an encounter between Renate Druks the real woman and Anaïs Nin.

Similarly, Tinguely's machine that destroys itself that appears at the exhibit that Mann, Sands and Renate attend at the end of the novel can be seen as a figure for the book. It is significant that as the machine (the novel?) destroys itself, Renate rescues the strip with the artists' names and the group of friends plans to repair to a bar to read the names to one another. *Collages* is itself a 'continuous novel.' It eddies around itself, proving the endlessly generative possibilities of art.

Hans, the painter from the story "The Eye's Journey" in *Under a Glass Bell* knows the lesson. He lives in his mind "at the bottom of the sea cluttered with objects from shipwrecks." Using these materials in his paintings he always paints a human eye in the corner of each one, "the secret door of his escape into the deep regions unknown."

Hans, unfortunately, cannot function as well in daily society. He hasn't paid rent in a year and lives in fear of being arrested or being served poisoned soup by the concierge, and he is sure the two men who have come to see him are there to steal his paintings and kill him.

The ability of the artist to have a vision at all is at stake in "The Eye's Journey." An artist who is so fixated on the internal and does not see the world around him at all for how it truly exists is no better than a man with a glass eye. But the artists in *Collages* know well how to connect the internal with the external and the novel itself, when seen along the earliest stories Nin wrote (now published as *Waste of Timelessness*) shows a sophisticated architecture of form from those stories through *House of Incest* and the more polished stories of *Under a Glass Bell*, and the novellas of both versions of *Winter of Artifice*. One could see all these books being published in a single volume to conclude with *Ladders to Fire* and the last four novels of *Cities of the Interior* joining *Collages* in a second full volume. Then the full range of Nin's achievements as a fiction writer could be more clearly seen.

Diane Richard-Allerdyce also saw *Collages* as precisely that investigation between Nin's modernist approach to fiction and what would later follow: "*Collages* participates in the questioning of artistic categories and genre boundaries typical of Postmodern theory, even as Nin remained thoroughly Modern in her emphasis on structure as an organizing element in art." (Allerdyce, p. 139) Nin herself was candid about the connection. In *Novel of the Future* she writes, "By 1966 it was the experience of the novelist which helped me edit the diary. It was the fiction writer who knew when the tempo lagged, when details were trivial, when a description was a repetition" (*Novel of the Future*, p. 164).

Finally, at the end (and *Collages* does *feel* like an ending), Nin returns back to her original sources, life itself—in the novel's case, Renate's life, but finally Nin's own as depicted in the *Diary*—but always fiction and diary have their sources in one another, it is a two way street, as circular and multidirectional as the rivers of music Djuna traverses in her mind. ❖

Works cited

Hinz, Evelyn. *The Mirror and the Garden: Realism and Reality in the Writings of Anaïs Nin.* New York: Harcourt Brace Jovanovich, 1973.

Jason, Philip K. *Anaïs Nin and Her Critics.* Columbia, SC: Camden House, 1993.

Nin, Anaïs. *Cities of the Interior*, with an introduction by Sharon Spencer. Athens: Ohio University Press, 1980.

----. *Collages.* Denver: Swallow Press, 1964.

----. *House of Incest*, with photomontages by Val Telberg. Denver: Swallow Press, 1958.

----. *The Mystic of Sex: Uncollected Writings, 1931-1974.* Ed. Gunther Stuhlmann. Santa Barbara: Capra Press, 1995.

----. *The Novel of the Future.* Athens: Ohio University Press, 1968.

Richard-Allerdyce, Diana. *Anaïs Nin and the Remaking of the Self: Gender, Modernism and Narrative Identity.* Carbondale: Northern Illinois Press, 1998.

Kastoori Barua

Hysteria, Creativity and Identity

Anaïs Nin's quest for the self

Anaïs Nin is famous for her diaries and erotic writing. Apart from these two identities as a writer, she is also seen as a feminist. In this paper, I attempt to explore the feminist dimension of Nin through her autobiographical quest for identity, creativity, and fulfilment by using two of her diaries as texts, namely *Henry and June* and *Mirages*, spanning the years 1931-32 and 1939-47 respectively.[1] Through this study I intend to demonstrate how she exploits her talent for literary writing as a "direct" way of achieving self-actualization. The modality of diary-writing is used by Nin so that, while it evidently gives a literary expression to her life, the same expression also serves as a process of self-actualization. I characterize this double role as Nin's unique way of living her life, which amounts to living life *as* literature. This literary trajectory of self-realization through her decisions in life and continual attempts to psychoanalyze herself during an era when women's rights were still emerging from the shadow of patriarchy, is definitely a fertile area of feminist-psychoanalytic study. Keeping the feminist-psychoanalytic angle in view, I shall shed theoretical light on my study by drawing upon certain ideas and observations of Freud, Lacan, Irigaray, and Kristeva.

Nin's childhood: a point of creative self-exploration

What plays a decisive role in the psycho-sexual development of Nin's early life, with its enduring impact on her maturity, is the diktat of paternal prohibition, the Lacanian "Law of the Father," which is connected with the notion of "Name-of-the-Father." By the time Nin is in her late teens, she is not able to sustain any impressionable relationship with her mother, even though the mother is naturally the immediate love-object of the child. Her Oedipal aspiration towards the mother is lastingly thwarted by her father's prohibitive intervention, and her own decisions in life. This forbidding intervention is what Lacan calls the symbolic father who acts as a delegate of a social law, which he dubbed the "name of the father."[2] The early relation with her father is one of painful rejection, resulting in a life of desire and incompletion pursuing lost objects, i.e., her father, love, adoration, etc. This lack of plenitude, of the wholeness and fullness of early childhood, while undergoing the process of prohibition and denial, amounts to the Lacanian equivalent of castration in Nin's case.

Notwithstanding the rejection of her by her father Joaquín Nin, and despite her mother's effort to the contrary, Anaïs the child takes on his name and identifies herself as Anaïs Nin (unlike her brother Joaquín Nin-Culmell, who includes his mother's surname). Significantly, the "symbolic" adoption of the father's surname for her formal identification acts as an outer and public ritual for her strong inner identification with her father. Nin's introjective identification with her father has an overwhelming influence on her finding an individual space, as a human subject, in the universe of meaning. As she enters the realm of the symbolic, she substitutes the "desire of the mother" for the "name of the father" (the "symbolic father" who upholds the symbolic order), which assumes the figure of law, legislating paternal prohibition. This is how she is initiated into the process of Lacanian castration.[3]

In Nin's case, this castration is related to the fact that she never develops any impressionable relationship with her mother, and that the pre-Oedipal mother-daughter relationship is sacrificed. In both *Henry and June* and *Mirages*, Nin never mentions anything significant about her mother, other than rarely referring to her mother's helpless pleas to her father to refrain from beating the children, and later referring to her living as a dependent of Anaïs and her husband Hugh (Hugo) Guiler. In contrast, Joaquín Nin remains quite visible in the diary entries in both books. Nin's relationship with her mother, which is initially quite close, deteriorates after Nin rebels against domestic chores as a teen, rejects the Church, marries a Protestant, and especially when she writes a book on D.H. Lawrence. There is a strong sense of disapproval that shadows the mother-daughter bond for the rest of their days. Thus, Nin's relationship with her mother becomes a casual and distant one, leaving no opportunity to develop into a deep mother-daughter nexus. It is a classic case of the suppression of the mother-daughter relationship that Irigaray highlights in her strand of psychoanalytic feminism.[4]

This genealogical asymmetry (i.e., the father-daughter relation without the mother-daughter relation) facilitates a split of the child's identity constituted of its pre-thetic sense of corporeal unity with the mother. This primal unity is thus ruptured in a thetic break leading to the inception of patriarchy, according to which, little girls are expected to become appealing visual objects and mirrors of men's desires. This break leads to the creation of subjectivity in the child in relation to the imaginary father.[5] The relation of the child here cannot be with the mother since she is a part of the child in the Lacanian pre-mirror stage. Hence the child cannot identify or differentiate the mother from itself. Since the bond of identification formed with the imaginary father is also the primary separation of the ego and the other, the "otherness" of the father, or the object-relation to the father, becomes the invitation to language. This momentous separation is the dawn of subjectivity in the child, which enables the child (subject) to have relationships with others.

It is precisely this gift of language which comes with the thetic break that Nin uses to win back her father. Nin's first diary, which begins at the age of eleven, was originally intended to be a letter to bring her father back to her. Language becomes her primary way of attempting at individuation and creative self-transformation. However, her attempts become somewhat futile due to the unintended penetration of a masculinized subjectivity, which is inherent in language. Subjectivity becomes masculinized as soon as female children are initiated into language (the symbolic order). In other words, the girl child becomes feminized because words constituting the woman are always in reference to masculinity, as complementary and reciprocal in their identities in relation to the man. This secures her in a masculine universe. Furthermore, the woman is assigned, by default, to a maternal destiny as mothers of men (and not of women). This happens due to the exclusion of the mother-daughter genealogy. Viewed from this theoretical explanatory standpoint, it is understandable why Nin in her forties acts as a mother to all her lovers, fulfilling their needs but unable to fulfill her own.

Search for identity: conflicting, creative, pleasurable

Nin's early adoption of the symbolic identity of her father was too entrenched in her psyche to facilitate the formation of an independent identity that she wants throughout her life. This conflictual situation makes her ongoing search for identity intense and poignant. As she grapples with her lost identity, she is not satisfied with the male-centered symbolic and cultural world where a woman is represented either as an "angel" or a "monster"—two mythical figures that represent the opposite ends of the spectrum of social norms in the human world.[6] Interestingly, she manages to transcend these two antithetical archetypal images by a curious conflation, and thereby assimilation, of both the images in order to create her own identity, her unique space. She writes:

> I will always be the virgin-prostitute, the perverse angel, the two-faced sinister and saintly woman. (*Henry and June*, p. 2)

This act of conflation of two antithetical concepts can be deemed as an act of rejecting the female aesthetic ideal set by men, who have fixed women at two ends of the kaleidoscope of society. Nin gives voice to the real woman who is a combination of both the ideal and the villainous. Alternatively, this ambiguous, dyadic identification can be read as the representation of her conflicting natures and desires, and the multiplicity of dispersed drives. Still not content with this synergetic constitution of herself as the virgin-cum-prostitute and sinister-cum-saintly, she turns to cultivating literary, artistic creativity as a means to define and form her identity. In *Henry and June*, she wants to be cognizant about what she has lived through—but as a poet, not as a psychoanalyst.

Driven by the force that Freud characterizes as the Pleasure Principle, Nin is constantly turning away from the pain of her childhood by pursuing that which gives her pleasure.[7] Freudian theory states three ways of seeking pleasure: powerful deflections like scientific activities, substitutive satisfactions, and intoxicating substances. Nin indulges in substitutive satisfactions, primarily engaging with art. Seeking beauty becomes a defense mechanism against pain and unhappiness. Nin finds beauty in the form and gestures of Henry Miller's wife, June, and in Miller's genius as a writer. Comfortable in this pursuit and mode of seeking pleasure and evading pain, she begins to see life as literature—as art. Seeing life as literature becomes a leitmotif running through her life henceforth.

Narrative identity, immortality and life as literature

Nin has the habit of turning personal incidents into life-spans. For instance, her passionate involvement with June, whom she loved like a proverbial Latin lover, is one that she lived through and died with. Such compartmentalized identities find their literary depiction in her creative works in the form of certain characters (e.g. Sabina, Lillian, Djuna, Stella, Hedja). Thus, by transplanting real-life incidents in the narrative space of literature, Nin turns her life in quest for identity into a life transfigured as literature.

Ardently intent on artistically creating herself through her passionate involvement with others, Nin becomes a protean creature whose power to recreate herself is invested in the intimate association with the men in her life. She reiterates that she *is* art as she goes on perpetuating art through her lived and imagined experiences. In the process of rendering herself as art, she commits herself to an emotionally extravagant life of hysterical indulgence bordering on decadence. Her sexual relationship with Henry Miller (described in *Henry and June*) is a hysterical emotional involvement aimed at finding fulfillment. Here, hysteria does not mean the wrongly identified age-old female-related problem of emotional excess because of the uterus that patriarchy has conveniently used to subdue women. Rather, it means the emotional excess that can take up various forms of manifestations such as writing, sexual intercourse etc. Hysteria, in this sense, is a constructive emotional frenzy that leads to creation.

Is one not perplexed by the idea of a life that *is* art even when this life is highlighted by hysterical frenzy? There is something puzzling about a life of creative hysterical frenzy *also* being a life of artistic creativity. One might suspect that there is an intrinsic conflict between art and the life of passionate frenzy, because the subject in emotional excess is likely to suffer loss of power of creative agency necessary for art. Although the creative expression of emotional excess may involve free play of the imagination, this kind of frenzied imagination is unlikely to be constructive of something that has the *unity* of a work of art, which is by definition a well-organized artifact. Therefore, the whole idea of a life of hysteria aspiring to become a life transfigured into art might strike us as dubious.

Besides, art involves artifice as a means of creating and entering into the realm of the artificial. More importantly, the imagination of artistic creativity becomes successfully constructive only when the artist knows how to negotiate with the artificial realm. This ability for negotiating with the artificial realm presupposes the artist's self-conscious grounding in the natural order of existence, thus making the artist at once a partaker of both the natural and the artificial order of being. But the subject of a life of hysteria, or of heightened moments of emotional frenzy, is unlikely to be in a position to negotiate with the imaginary order in the same manner as the artist of controlled imagination. And it is more unlikely that this subject is in a position to partake of the imaginary order simultaneously with the life of the natural order. What is problematic in this case is whether the subject of hysterical passion can afford to adopt the attitude of "aesthetic distance" required for artistic negotiation with the imaginary realm. And the adequacy of aesthetic distance from the natural order, a kind of withdrawal from one's engaged existential stance, so persuasively advocated by Kant and Schopenhauer amongst others, certainly presupposes a certain amount of *dispassionate* rational control of imagination.[8]

We therefore need to clear the oxymoronic air out of the idea of "hysterical creativity" or "creative hysteria" thematically used in attempting to understand Nin's quest for self-identity. Nin's hysteria must be complex enough to demand a layered understanding, a kind of structured probing through the surface of those unwieldy passions, so that we can identify what actually runs, as a subterranean current of rational thought and intention, beneath the apparent frenzy. What shows on the surface are bouts of anxiety and illness, which are most often that of her feeling extremely put out when her lovers cancel a tryst (e.g., when Bill Pinckard or Gore Vidal fails to come to her home). But could the cancelation of such a tryst have repercussions of such a severe nature? One may think that the reactions of emotional extremity of the kind that she had need to be explained in a more nuanced way than the usual psychological explanation of hysterical frenzy.

It can arguably be conjectured, therefore, that there is, on Nin's part, an unconscious willful manipulation of her own emotional state. Deep down in her psyche, she engages in the unconscious strategy of provoking herself to a point of frenzy, so that compelling passions motivate her to literary creativity. Her obsessive passions are so heightened that hysterical outbursts are purposively converted into facilitators of creative artistic self-expression. This means, of course, that her hysteria cannot be unproblematically categorized as what usually happens to a hysterical subject. Indeed, she is far from consistently being a victim of hysteria. Her case seems to be psychologically unusual, inasmuch as there is a fairly strong undercurrent of intent that structures her hysteria into a goal-directed reactive disposition, which is the disposition to configure life into art. It is this intent or purposive stance, latent or hidden though it is, that is cunningly operative in Nin's negotiation with the imaginary and artistic ordering of her life.

Thus the hysterical mode of self-constitution and quest for identity marks Nin's life with extremities of heightened love, arousing passion both in her lovers and in herself. But the underlying reason for such an emotionally extravagant quest for identity is, of course, the haunting memory of her utterly neglected childhood, which explains why she is constantly and desperately trying to draw passionate attention from her lovers. This is a strategy of her trying to prove to herself that she is no longer the unimpressionable child-Anaïs who was repeatedly spurned by her father. Also, this penchant for arousing passion is in fact her will to outgrow the past and overcome the habit of obsessive introspection. In an effort to escape from disconcerting self-awareness, she seeks interest in numerous social engagements (such as attending parties with her friends, going to bordellos with Hugo, etc.) and creative writing. It is much later, a decade after the phase of *Henry and June*, in the phase of *Mirages*, that she is able to attain the passion that she yearns for.

The memory of a traumatic childhood of being neglected and abandoned by her father creates an agonizing fear of abandonment in her, subjecting her many a time to extreme anxiety and psychosomatic illness (hysteria). Hence she resorts to the creative life of writing as a way of overcoming anxiety and preventing disintegration, thereby coming to terms with finitude and mortality by a mythic intimation of immortality in an awareness of "cosmic consciousness." She acknowledges:

> I write too, because creation is my way of reaching the "cosmic consciousness" of the mystics, because this highest point of my being is the point which survives and continues, and I knew my highest self is the one who will not die. (*Mirages*, p. 93)

This mysticism of "cosmic consciousness" is certainly not the ultimate end for her. Scared of living a banal life with no spotlight on herself, Nin wants to live out a life of excess and passions, which is essentially geared to making literature out of life through her talent for mythmaking. With her mythic eye, she tends to see in each person the elemental, larger-than-life characteristics. She pulls them back to earthy primitivism. She calls Allendy, her psychoanalyst (in *Henry and June*), the child of men who sailed the seas; Miller is called the Demon of Literature; Edward Graeffe is called Siegfried; Gonzalo becomes the son of the Inca Sun gods (*Mirages*, p. 61). Presumably she has a kind of "mythopoeic" urge to symbolize the men in her life, and giving them names or titles are born of this urge.

The myth-making imagination with which Nin creates for herself a sense of immortality in her mortal life is perhaps the best way she can hope to be remembered for her choices, and for her surprising rigidity. She wants to immortalize the significance of her creative choices as a woman who struggles to establish an identity in a world basically shaped by patriarchy. This longing for immortality, or the desire to be remembered for her choices, is *her* way of registering the voice of feminism. Nin is evocatively expressive of her ardent intention: "I want to leave the feminine scar." (*Henry and June*, p. 225)

But why would she desire to register the voice of feminism in the pejorative guise of a "scar"? The answer is to be found in her rebellious reaction against patriarchy, on both social and linguistic levels. This ironically characterized phrase is intended to be a radical subversion of male-centric linguistic construal of women as "devilish" when they challenge the norms of patriarchy. Leaving the feminine scar was her way of disfiguring the structure of the male-centric language within which she, like all other women, is forced to operate.

Nin gives a perspicuous expression to the legacy of the "feminine scar" in the actual or putative lives of three illustrious women, one mythical and the other two real: Helen of Troy, Virginia Woolf and Rebecca West, respectively.[9] These women were either childless or had strained relationships with their children, and contrary to the patriarchal expectation, these women lived their lives by their own terms. Thus, to leave the feminine scar is to register the abiding effect of being a woman who demonstrates her unique identity through her independent and resolute choices. Hence, the feminine scar is quite literally a disfiguration of the tapestry of patriarchy, and Nin wants to contribute to this longstanding legacy. It is also important to add that the woman leaves the feminine scar by her choice to live as someone who makes her womanhood independent of the burden of motherhood imposed by patriarchy. Thus, Nin deftly critiques patriarchy which has debased motherhood into becoming an existential burden.

Nin, the mother: a contradictory desire

Exasperated at having to give in to the continuous demands of the men in her passionate life, Nin complains: "Each day there are more demands from me that deprive me of the liberty I need" (*Henry and June*, p. 262). She then gains a sense of an imperceptible autonomy that makes her search for identity no longer utterly dependent on others, and she no longer wants to be protected or have her frailty highlighted. But, paradoxically, she also wants men to make enormous demands on her, so that she can prove herself to them a complete woman. It is as though she is struggling to outgrow the child in her by meeting these self-imposed demands, so that she can be treated as a woman of her own standing.

However, this desire for autonomy betrays Nin's constant narcissistic need for the validation of her self-importance. Believing that she can prove her importance only by doing what she considers to be grand and impossible, she chooses to fall in love with tempestuous men, e.g., Henry and Gonzalo. Her eventual migration from Paris to New York is followed by her obsessive thirst for young lovers. This obsession with young/child lovers is, for Nin, an unconscious desire to become the archetypal Mother, bent on providing everything for her sons.

An interesting contradiction arises when we compare her desire to be a mother to her "child"-lovers with her desire to leave the "feminine scar" on the world. These two desires are at best mutually incompatible; having the latter desire satisfied would mean forsaking the former desire, and vice versa. At the root of this incompatibility of desires is her inefficacious struggle to reconcile the idealized identity of a woman with the real woman of mortal frailty that she is. That frailty shows itself in what can arguably be said to be her ambivalent attitude towards motherhood. Presumably, her overriding need for espousing motherhood is at bottom a selfish one. While she "plays" the mother out of her obsessive desire and firm commitment to mold her child-lovers into ideal mature men, she is motivationally incapable of any commitment to having a child of her own and rearing it with the same patience and perseverance.

The shift from France to America is one of the defining moments in Nin's life. With a defiant sense of creative urge set against the perceived creative aridity of America in the 1940s, she becomes a writer of deeper and somber prose, increasingly philosophical, penetratingly introspective, and imaginatively allusive. Outgrowing her need to seek external validation of her beauty, she now comes to believe that people will look in her for a deeper connection—a universal connection that is akin to the "oceanic" feeling that Freud talks about in *Civilization and its Discontents*. This is the beginning of Nin's self-apotheosis. This oceanic feeling is traced back to the early phase of ego-feeling stemming from the helplessness and need of the father's protection during childhood. Nin becomes a Mother-figure, displacing the rigid Father-figure and nurturing and protecting her child-lovers so that they grow up to be mature men.

Split of the adult and the child/artist

It is ironic that, although Nin seeks out youth, passion, and abundance in her young loves, what she really wants is the mature man, whom she wants to create for herself through these young lovers' pulsating veins of life. She instills in her lovers a creativity that was either lacking or dormant in them. She believes that the process of maturation is more important and of greater value than the final outcome. But, unlike Kristeva's loving mother who provides the first approach to language and law to her child by demonstrating love for an object who is not the child, Nin does not bring any serious third party into her relationships with her child-lovers.[10] By eliminating the loving father who encourages the child to represent itself while disrupting its fusion with the mother by virtue of its own existence, Nin becomes a mother whose only object of desire is her child. Thus, she ultimately produces children who cannot move beyond the psychosis of being the phallus for her. Their limitation finally makes Nin grow out of them.

Indeed, creation through words is the key to Nin's liberation. Each of her books has brought a new man to her life. Through her works she seeks the man, and through the man she attains fulfillment. So she writes in self-admonition:

> Create, Anaïs. Every word you wrote was always the golden key which opened the doors of your prison. The Lawrence book brought you Henry. The *House of Incest* brought you Gonzalo. *The Winter of Artifice* John [Dudley]. It is your female chant for man, for the lover. Write. It is your ornament, your grace, your seduction, your chant for courting. (*Mirages*, p. 30)

This sustained process of self-addressing, a reflexive speech-act that Nin performs from time to time, can arguably be considered as a distinctive mode of self-creation. But her identity-formation consists of two strands: one is of literary creativity through self-addressing, and the other of becoming a confirmed beloved of the truly mature man. Although both the strands are interconnected in the unfolding of her life, the nature of this intersection subsequently complicates, post-*Henry and June*, her life. But the earlier phase is dominated by the pursuit of erotic passion. Even this phase is not free from complication. She develops a kind of split personality because of her conflicting desire for young lovers and at the same time wanting them to be mature men. In fact, the adult and the child/artist within her are at friction, and there needs to be a synthesis, or the friction overcome, for the sake of attaining the phallus (fulfillment).

Later on, Nin ceases to consider erotic passion as the absolute, and conceives of her fulfillment in terms of the organic fusion of the sensual and the intellectual, the earthy and the mystical. This is anticipated when she writes in her diary: "Why must I suffer so deeply in my earthly loves and find joy only in the mystical ones?" (*Mirages*, p. 44).

Realization: realizing the self

One of the most significant points of departure in her frantic search for identity is the definitive break with Miller, whose world-view is now radically incompatible with her own. Besides, she comes to see how, just for the sake of helping Miller realize his dreams, she has reduced herself from being an avid dreamer of higher fulfillment to a plain realist, a mere human being, basically providing material support to his life. With her forsaking of Miller, the legend of *Tristan and Iseult* is laid to rest, as it were, with Iseult falling out of love.[11]

At this juncture, the following admission on Nin's part is significant: "While man's tendency is to be born, to emerge, woman's is to take back, to keep, to contain" (*Mirages*, p. 144). What is suggested here is Nin's perception of the binary ideas of sexual identity, of men and women in society. She reaches Kristeva's idea of the "cyclic time" through the symbolic realm of the female (the womb) when expressed in terms of space and repetition. Kristeva argues that female subjectivity presents itself in repetition and eternity rather than in linear temporality. Given their monthly periods, pregnancies and births, they are attuned to the world of nature, the changing seasons: "there are cycles, gestation, the eternal recurrence of a biological rhythm which conforms to that of nature..."[12] This is in contrast to man's attunement to "time as project, teleology, linear and prospective unfolding; time as departure, progression, and arrival—in other words, the time of history."[13] Hence they can move forward, achieve things with ease and less suffering, whereas women are held down by their biological qualities of retention and repetition.

Nin realizes that even though she has rejected motherhood, she still behaves like the archetypal mother to all her lovers, thus impeding her own growth. In a way, Nin was grappling with a way of living by "reaching beyond" biologically constrained temporality. In this regard, she anticipates Kristeva's emphasis on the multiplicity of female conditions, expressions, tendencies and preoccupations in a bid to "break the code, to shatter language, to find a specific discourse closer to the body and emotions, to the unnamable repressed by the social contract."[14] By opting out of motherhood, she breaks the biological cycle of repetition and retention, thus considering this to be the only way of moving forward during her time.

At this point of her breaking away from her young lovers, Nin realizes that the father figure that she has so long resented and avenged herself on is what she herself is now. She is the female Don Juan.[15] The hairline difference between Joaquín Nin and herself is that the former is propelled by desire, whereas she is propelled both by desire and love. Once again, she takes the place of the father in the symbolic order. She is now a composite creature, a dialectical being mythical in proportion.

Cities of the interior: negotiation and loss

Nin creates her own technique of distorting the picture of the real world by supplanting it with her own world and fixes herself in a state of psychical infantilism, finally succeeding in sparing herself of an individual neurosis. Her creation is private, complex, delicate, and prone to fallibility from externalities that constantly threaten to converge on her world and destroy it. She admits this in her diary:

> I give myself mystical explanations of my roles and destiny, mystical reasons for my sacrifices. I hold a romantic image of myself as from another world. It is this self I fear to open to the world, because when I do give it, open it to all, it gets shattered. (*Mirages*, p. 274)

Since she must protect her world, Nin interacts cautiously with the outside world, trying to merge the two to a degree of mutual complicity, and free the former from any kind of threat.

It is only after a string of doomed love affairs that she realizes that her child-lovers cannot progress into maturity even when she pours her love and passion into them. It is at this crucial juncture that Nin is significantly transformed by a reflective self-understanding about her bodily passions and longing for the child-lovers. This passionate longing has until now been more of an *intra*-subjective and one-way desire for love and fulfillment, with herself as the central subject, a self-enclosed egoist architect who designs the project of love and fulfillment in terms more of her own than of the other. With this self-transformative realization she now thinks in terms of *inter*-subjective relationality, convinced that the desired and intended lover enjoys no less centrality in the mutual project of love and fulfillment.

In this self-realization Nin comes to understand the body as a "player" in this real-life game of love. Although the body is one's own and thus irreducibly a personal possession, it is not a private object that can be, as it were, deployed in an act of establishing a relationship merely in terms of one's own subjectivity and ego-centric aspirations, all ensconced in one's self-created world of desire. On the contrary, the personal body must also play a "social" role in the sense of being willing to meet an "inter-personal" obligation, which means that the other body of desire and intention is as much at stake as one's own. In other words, the condition of reciprocity that applies to a true relationship is not just an abstract idea, but an essential ingredient of bodily inter-subjectivity and interpersonal fulfillment.

This self-transformative realization about inter-subjective relationality transforms Nin's world-view so much so that she not only relinquishes her compulsive desire for younger men but even breaks out of the cyclic nature of women, in order to move to new spaces altogether.[16] Nin's eventual but enduring settlement with Rupert Pole is a testimony to this momentous break. Pole was at once able to satisfy the dialectical components of Nin's nature—that of the mystic and the sensualist, the child/artist and the adult. Through the mature man, and by relinquishing a part of her internal world, Nin is finally able to integrate the dialectical signifiers of her identity and become whole and fulfilled.

Conclusion

The trajectory of Nin's life is hysterical in the psychoanalytic sense of the term. Her act of creative writing about her own life is simultaneously an act of constructing her own identity and conferring meaning on life. This constructive act of identity formation is intensely experimental, and the experiment is hysterically tumultuous inasmuch as it involves many contradictions and regressions. However, she ultimately manages to break out of the "cyclic nature" of the woman she is. This break is crucially dependent on her realized transition, in her search for identity and fulfillment, and from the intra-subjective matrix of desire to the level of inter-subjective relationality. The hysterical zeal for identity and fulfillment carries no guarantee of success even if it is undertaken as a creative experimental enterprise. It is therefore significant that Nin's autobiographical experimental self-exploration in the messy world of love and aspiration culminates in reasonable contentment. More significant, perhaps, is the question of how feminist constraints and confrontations shape the contours of this passionate experiment with life. ❖

Notes

1 Anaïs Nin, consolidated and unexpurgated diaries charting 1931-32 in *Henry and June* published by Harcourt, and 1939-47 in *Mirages* by Sky Blue Press/Swallow Press.

2 The idea of the "Law of the Father" with its cognate notion of "Name of the Father" suggesting the role of the father in the symbolic order is developed by Lacan in *The Seminar of Jacques Lacan, Book III: The Psychoses*, trans. Russell Grigg, edited by Jacques-Alain. Miller (New York: Norton: 2000), to cover the role of the father in the Symbolic Order. A more elaborate account is given in Jacques Lacan, *On the Names-of-the-Father*, trans. by Bruce Fink (Cambridge: Polity Press, 2013).

3 The idea of castration formulated by Lacan interestingly differs from that of Freud, as does the related idea of the "phallus" in contrast to the Freudian notion of penis. Lacanian castration does not refer to the biological organ, but to the imaginary and symbolic notion of phallus, which points towards a system of signifiers. What concerns psychoanalytic theory, for Lacan, is not the male genital organ in its biological reality, but the role this organ plays in fantasy—the imaginary and symbolic functions of this organ. Castration is defined as a symbolic lack of an imaginary object. As a symbolic element, as the signifier of the other's desire, the phallus could potentially be an infinite number of possible things.

A concise description of "castration complex" is to be found in Dylan Evans, *An Introductory Dictionary of Lacanian Psychoanalysis*, (London & New York: Routledge, 1996), pp. 22-24.

4 Luce Irigaray, *Speculum of the Other Woman*, translated by Gillian C. Gill, (Ithaca, NY: Cornell University Press, 1985).

5 This idea of the "imaginary father," who is essentially loving in nature in contrast to the Freudian and Lacanian idea of the fear-inducing authoritarian father-figure, is propounded by Julia Kristeva in *Tales of Love*, tr. by Leon S. Roudiez (New York: Columbia University Press, 1987). Classical psychoanalysis views the father as an authoritarian figure threatening the child with the fear of castration. This loss/erosion of the loving father is the reason for psychic discontent. Against this crisis in paternity, Kristeva tries to recover a loving father by focusing on the absent paternal body. The child is left as bereft of love due to the reduction of the mother to a body and of the father to that of a distant social authority. Against this erosion of love, Kristeva's feminist strategy is to construct the figure of the imaginary father, who allows the child to dissociate itself from its mother and yet remain loved by this imaginary father. Thus, the imaginary father is a feminist psychoanalytic antidote to the stern "Law of the Father."

[6] Sandra Gilbert and Susan Gubar, *The Madwoman in the Attic: The Woman Writer and Nineteenth-Century Literary Imagination*, 2nd edition (New Haven, CT: Yale University Press, 2000).

[7] Sigmund Freud, *Civilization and its Discontents*, translated by David McLintock (London: Penguin Books, 2002).

[8] Immanuel Kant's idea of aesthetic disinterestedness is a central theme in his *Critique of the Power of Judgement*, trans. by Paul Guyer and Eric Mathews (Cambridge: Cambridge University Press, 2000). Arthur Schopenhauer's conception of the aesthetic attitude is articulated in terms of what he calls aesthetic contemplation, in virtue of which we are able to experience the world as representation rather than as will or desire. See Arthur Schopenhauer, *The World as Will and Representation*, Volume I, trans. E. F. J. Payne (New York: Dover, 1969).

[9] For an account of the "feminine scar," please refer to Anaïs Nin and Henry Miller, *A Literate Passion 1932-1953*, edited by Gunther Stuhlmann (New York: Harcourt Brace & Company, 1987), p. 99.

[10] In *In the Beginning was Love: Psychoanalysis and Faith* (New York: Columbia University Press, 1987), Julia Kristeva, writes: "The loving mother...has an Other with relation to whom the child will serve as a go-between... She will love her child with respect to that Other [i.e., the child's father], ...that Third Party" (p. 34). That is, no mother-child couple exists without a symbolic father somewhere.

[11] *Tristan and Iseult* is a Celtic legend about the tragic adulterous love between Cornish knight Tristam and the Iris princess Iseult.

[12] Julia Kristeva, "Women's Time," *Signs: Journal of Women in Culture and Society*, vol. 7, no. 1, 1981, p. 16.

[13] *Ibid.*, p. 17.

[14] *Ibid.*, pp. 24-25. Rejecting the feminism that had become too codified and restrictive, Kristeva argues, in her article "Women's Time," for the arrival of the "Third Wave" of feminism that will create its own signifying space and enable the imposition of its own definitions of human identity by overthrowing and reconstructing binary ideas on sexual identity. This new position involves a deconstructive approach to sexual difference, rejecting the dichotomy of masculine and feminine as metaphysical.

[15] This Don Juan does not refer to Lord Byron's eponymously titled satiric poem. It refers to the character coined by Tirso de Molina (Gabriel Tellez) in *The Trickster of Seville and the Stone Guest.*

[16] In Nin's case, the "cyclic nature" refers to the repeated way in which she was engaged in the process of finding fulfillment in her young lovers. It is of course clear that this phrase (of Kristeva) is being used metaphorically to highlight Nin's circular trajectory of doom with young lovers.

Jean Owen

The Sting of Incest

Kathryn Harrison's father-romance in The Kiss

I am beginning to know what it means: *unspeakable*—Kathryn Harrison

Kathryn Harrison's troubling memoir *The Kiss* (1997)[1] is not the usual rite of passage story from innocence to knowledge: it is a journey from early childhood abandonment to carnal knowledge of the father, which renders it similar—though not straightforwardly—to that of Anaïs Nin's father romance as depicted in *Incest* (1992).[2] In an interview with Harrison I asked whether she was aware of Nin's unexpurgated diary, which tells of her reunion and eventual incestuous affair with her father after a twenty-year absence.[3] She responded:

> It has been many years—25—since I have read anything by Anaïs Nin, whose work I sought out in my early 20s, hoping for some form of enlightenment—rescue, even. I don't remember much of her work, other than that I found it incredible—not believable—that she characterized her sexual relationship with her father as not injurious. At least, that's how I remember it.

It is an intriguing comment, given that Harrison is referring to a period when Nin's sexual relationship with her father was only implicit. Indeed, the full import of her incestuous encounter was only realized in 1992, when the unexpurgated volume was published, five years before Harrison's own memoir. Harrison's use of the emotive term "unbelievable" in response to what she claims to be Nin's characterization of incest as "not injurious" is odd, too, given that Nin herself has never made that claim. Indeed, she frequently commented that without psychoanalysis, she would have continually repeated the "father cycle" (the quest for the lost father) in her writings.[4]

There are uncanny resemblances between Nin's *Incest* and Harrison's *The Kiss* besides their recreation of the closed-off world of incest, not least because both books have their fictionalized counterparts—*The Winter of Artifice* (first published in 1939) and *Thicker Than Water* (1991)—which were written and published earlier and are significantly different in relation to their portrayal of incest.[5] Interestingly, too, there is a history of editing *The Kiss* that contains an echo of Nin's re-editing process. Harrison writes: "In essence, I'd struggled for a decade with the fact that I had an 'unspeakable' story to tell. I knew it was a story I wasn't supposed to tell, but I also knew I wouldn't be able to develop as a writer, or do anything of value with the rest of my life, until I did tell it" (*The Kiss*, p. 220). In this sense, and in line with Nin's incest narrative, *The Kiss* becomes something of a *Künstlerroman*, a genre that depicts a writer's growth to artistic maturity and forms part of the writer's (as much as the narrator's) resolution of a rite of incest.

There are other similarities that warrant brief comment before I look in detail at *The Kiss*. Nin and Harrison align their respective heroines Anaïs and Kathryn with female figures from a range of literary sources (though Harrison more so): Lilith, Alraune, and a Don Juana for Nin (though she cast herself, and anagrams her name, in ways more inventive than this list implies), Lot's daughters for both of them, and Electra, Sleeping Beauty, St. Dympna and St. Catherine, among others for Harrison. Both writers stage their confessions as a quest narrative in mythic terms, although Harrison tends towards the more tragic, since there isn't the hint of humor in her narrative that is to be found in Nin's. Harrison also draws on motifs from folklore, including a kiss and golden hair. There is the idea of a twenty-year separation for both of them, though Kathryn is just six months old when her father leaves, whereas Anaïs is ten years old, just as Kathryn is only twenty when the relationship with her father begins, some ten years younger than Anaïs is in Nin's account. And while Kathryn's "affair" with her father lasts four years, Anaïs's lasts nine months.

Turning now to the particulars of *The Kiss*: Kathryn's parents are both eighteen when they meet during their senior year of high school. An out-of-wedlock pregnancy and subsequent marriage without money or prospects means that the adolescent couple are forced to live with her maternal grandparents. Shortly after giving birth, the young mother has a nervous breakdown. This gives the grandparents a chance to get rid of the unwanted son-in-law by bribing him to leave the baby in their care, and so the newlyweds divorce when Kathryn is only six months old. Thereafter her father becomes a distant figure, and she is not allowed to mention him. His absence is felt more keenly by the child due to her grandmother's practice of editing her father out of family photographs. She sees him only twice during her childhood, both occasions proving disastrous.

When Kathryn is six, her mother moves out of the family home to her own apartment, thus relinquishing any daily care of the doubly abandoned daughter. Meanwhile Kathryn's father, determined to prove his worth, secures himself a doctorate, becomes a church minister, remarries and has three other children, none of whom know of his first family until Kathryn turns up at the age of twenty.

On her twentieth birthday Kathryn is reunited with her father when he stays as a guest at her mother's apartment. At the airport, as he is about to leave, he gives her a kiss that splits her world in two. Before long he has seduced her into a sexual relationship which is to last a feverish four years, during which time they meet in seedy motels and other marginal places to satisfy their mutual obsession. Only when Kathryn's mother is dying of cancer and the remorseful daughter places her recently shorn princess hair on the sickbed in a perverse ritual of sacrifice does the father-romance finally end.

Harrison's father-romance is a quest for the lost father, but also includes a quest for the lost mother, which isn't the case for Nin. Kathryn's father-hunger is inseparable from—indeed it is a correlative of—the mother-hunger the abandoned daughter feels. As Harrison presents it, the intricate and irrevocably destructive relationship of daughter and mother is *the* driving force behind the daughter-father liaison. It is the mother who links daughter to father in their pursuit of what Kathryn perceives as their shared lost love object. In other words,[6] what brings daughter and father together is their rivalry for the mother. Kathryn is a wronged daughter in a way Anaïs isn't: she feels neglected and rejected by her mother to the point where she has been excluded from the latter's life and so looks for love elsewhere. In doing so, she finds a means of exacting revenge in the spirit of an Electra. In response to my enquiry about the Freudian theme, Harrison comments

> My relationship with my father cannot be teased out from my relationship with my mother, and I wouldn't want to rely on one construct—like "Electra Complex"—to explain my behaviour. Certainly I needed to know my father, to experience his love for me. I also was violently, destructively, angry with my mother, and the relationship my father offered me allowed me to punish her. (Owen/Harrison interview)

Quite clearly, Kathryn is more preoccupied with her mother—in fact, she remains *the* primary object—and uses her father to get to her, just as Electra does.[7] When the mother suspects that something sexual is going on between Kathryn and her father, for instance, she takes her to a (actually, the mother's) psychiatrist in an attempt to extract a confession. To add insult to her mother's injury Kathryn, who normally clothes herself in black, baggy clothes, wears the most inappropriate outfit—a very short tight purple dress and high heels. Without any preamble, the mother tells the doctor that she thinks daughter and father are having sex. When confronted with the accusation, Kathryn answers

> "It just looks bad [...] I know why she's worried. But...it's just that..." I falter. "See, I never knew my father. I'm going through a stage, like all little girls, just later than most."
>
> I pause at exactly the right moments. My performance is so good that I'm frightened. Is my personality so unformed that putting on a dress is enough to change it? Or is this shameless, sexual, purple-clad girl—someone I can't imagine as a friend—a part of me? "She's right," I say, nodding. "I am in love with him, but it...I'm not...I'd never...I wouldn't do that." (p. 142)

Kathryn's confession of a belated Electra complex is designed to destroy her mother's credibility in front of the doctor, which it does since both believe her: she clearly knows the theory she has, by this time, already put into practice. As with the wife/daughter doubling motif in incest folktales (though not because of their physical resemblance), the daughter has already replaced her mother *as daughter* to her grandmother; here, in a more treacherous move, she replaces her as the father's lover. At times, it is difficult to see where the mother ends and the daughter begins. They are extensions of each other, "loving" the same man in a copycat parallel that sees Kathryn masquerade her mother's adolescent behavior in "running off" with him after his first visit. But, of course, there is one fundamental difference: Kathryn's act is infinitely more transgressive since the stranger she is running off with her own father.[8] *The Kiss* exposes what Harrison calls the "fault lines" of the white middle class heterosexual family triangle, a visceral world of incest swarming beneath its vertices, lines of desire connecting parent to parent and parent to child. On the father's first visit, the newly united threesome spends a week at the mother's flat, parodying the idea of "happy families:"

> We try hard to make it work, the three of us together. We sit in the living room and drink iced tea. "At last," one of us says, "a family." Calling ourselves this, saying the words—Who says them? My mother? My father? Did I?—it's meant ironically, but the pain the words bring, the admission of failure, is so intense that afterward no one speaks. (p. 53)

On a second visit "that hard-won, precarious balance of our threesome, our 'little family,' has been undone" (p. 95). A triangle meant for bonding swiftly becomes one of competition, jealousy and rivalry as much as it becomes a vehicle for narcissistic identification and incest as father and daughter turn away from the mother and towards each other. At last the daughter takes centre-stage in her father's affections, ousting the mother and winning what seems to be the coveted prize, the (ex-) husband.

Harrison remarks: "I feel that what unfolded among me and my parents was an archetypal conflict, and I wanted to strip away much of what made us particular people" (Owen/Harrison interview). The "archetypal conflict" is, ostensibly, a triangulated (Oedipal and, thus, heterosexual) model of the family consisting of parent-parent-child and abstracted to its mythic essence. This gives *The Kiss* the distinctive flavor of a folktale with its intentionally "flat" characters. The folktale tends to define identity by role; in the main, characters have no names but exist, to some degree, as abstractions. The narrator, Kathryn, is the only character with a real name and thus the only real presence in the memoir (though she defines herself almost exclusively through her parents rather than as an autonomous individual); all other characters muster around the edges, giving the impression that they are somehow set apart from history, timeless, even mythic.

This atmosphere of timelessness is teased out in the theme of transition, which, as with any rite of passage (or in this case, rite of incest), is a significant part of Kathryn's experience: "[t]he road always stretches endlessly ahead and behind us, so that we are out of time as well as out of place" (p. 3). "Nowhere" is used as an organizing principle within *The Kiss* as daughter and father traverse America, a movement that has a strange, dislocating effect on the reader. In our interview, I suggested to Harrison that *The Kiss* is, in fact, evocative of the road movie genre such as Nabokov's *Lolita* in which (step) father and daughter upset the domestic environment of the family home by embarking on a journey where, as she says, the unreal location of "nowhere and notimes" is your only home. Harrison states:

> Nabokov recognized that the outlaw nature of incest required a father and daughter to take to the road—that there is no place for such relationships within the social contract; [our relationship] played itself out on the road, apart from our families, our places in the world. (Owen/Harrison interview)

This "in-between" space represents the outlawed state of a fugitive daughter and her father: for Kathryn, the father's return is supposed to rectify the earlier loss, and to enable the reshaping of the daughter's landscape; instead it leads to further separation and obsession that appear more brutal than anything presented by Nin. Interestingly, whereas in Nin's narrative of incest, Anaïs continues seeing a range of men, including her husband, Henry Miller and Otto Rank, in Harrison, incest cuts Kathryn off completely from all peers, all boyfriends.

Yet, as with Anaïs and Joaquín, in *The Kiss* daughter and father become mutually absorbed by each other and Kathryn, for the first time, enjoys her own sense of narcissism which, up to this point, had been the sole province of her mother: "My father looks at me, then, as no one has ever looked at me before. His hot eyes consume me [...] I almost feel their touch" (p. 51). Kathryn's father's eyes (an intriguing motif throughout the memoir) "burn like a prophet's, a madman's, a lover's" that "*see* me into being." In terms that seem to echo Anaïs's dilemma when she becomes involved with her father, Kathryn affirms

> Looking at him looking at me, I can't help but fall painfully, precipitously in love. And my loving him is inseparable from a piercing sense of loss [...] How can it be that I am twenty years old, that I've grown up without a father, only to meet him now when it's too late, when childhood is over, lost? (p. 63)

In sentimental romance fiction a girl's first kiss is something she never forgets; indeed, it marks *the* rite of passage towards sexual awakening. In *The Kiss*, Kathryn experiences a very different "first" kiss that sets her on a rite of incest. The life-changing kiss that gives the memoir its title takes place when Kathryn and her father say goodbye at the Los Angeles International Airport after that first reunion:

> With his hand under my chin, my father draws my face toward his own. He touches his lips to mine. I stiffen. I've seen it before: fathers kissing their daughters on the mouth. A friend of mine's father has kissed her that way for years, and I've watched them, unable to look away, disquieted by what I see. [...] As I pull away, feeling the resistance of his hand behind my head, how tightly he holds me to him, the kiss changes. It is no longer a chaste, closed-lipped kiss. My father pushes his tongue deep into my mouth: wet, insistent, exploring, then withdrawing. [...] I am frightened by the kiss. I know it's wrong, and its wrongness is what lets me know, too, that it is a secret. (pp. 67-69)

The inappropriateness of some father-daughter kisses has long fascinated Kathryn, but here the unnamed father enters forbidden territory—his daughter's mouth. It is the most intimately and publicly incongruous gesture he could make as the fledgling paternal gives way to the erotic. Yet it is not so much that the kiss brings about Kathryn's sexual awakening—she is not a virgin when she meets her father—rather, it seems to shut her down as Sleeping Beauty is shut down by the prick of a spindle:

> In years to come, I'll think of the kiss as a kind of transforming sting, like that of a scorpion: a narcotic that spreads from my mouth to my brain. The kiss is the point at which I begin, slowly, inexorably, to fall asleep, to surrender volition, to become paralyzed. (p. 71)

Kathryn's sting of incest is not fatal, but it is anesthetizing. In kissing his daughter as a lover would, the father places Kathryn under a spell, a slow poison that begins to separate her from everyone else and seems to be the real sexual transgression or at least the inaugural event that leads to full-blown incest. What should have been a simple "goodbye" to bring them closer together as father and daughter, actually separates them from notions of the proper family, and thus from society. Kathryn comments: "I have embarked on a peculiar passage in my life—a time out of real time, one which will not fit either into the life I lived as a child or the one I create as a woman, but which will carry me, like a road, from one to the other" (pp. 101-102). Kathryn's "peculiar passage" marks the threshold between life before the kiss and what unfolds after, on the road and in all those "unreal" places.

Aside from its function in folkloric terms, the kiss in the memoir is our entry into the incestuous relationship. This means that it is all too easy to cut it off from other incestuous encounters. Indeed, it can be somewhat misleading in terms of the daughter's desire for the father since it is *his* inappropriate behavior that is blamed for activating the incestuous relationship, unlike in Nin's account, where in the incest-acts are represented as more mutually seductive and pleasurable, if also highly ambiguous, and even poisonous. In *The Kiss*, when Kathryn finally gives in to her father's sexual demands during a trip in which she is introduced to her paternal family, "it is almost a relief" (p. 136). She comments: "After the agony of resistance, when for so long it's been clear that a fall is imminent, plummeting is a kind of fulfilment. I plunge without knowing how fast I fall or how far, how hard the bottom will be when I hit." She continues:

> In years to come, I won't be able to remember even one instance of our lying together. I'll have a composite, generic memory. I'll know that he was always on top and that I always lay still, as still as if I had, in truth, fallen from a great height [...] But I won't be able to remember what it felt like. No matter how hard I try, pushing myself to inhabit my past, I'll recoil from what will always seem impossible. (pp. 136-37)

Note the prim, biblical illusion to "lying together." I shall return to the subject of religion shortly. Here, I think, Harrison is referring to the actual physical sensation of the incest-act rather than the emotional state, which she certainly captures very well, including all the physical details of the incestuous surroundings and "every tiny thing about" her father.

> [W]hen my father comes quietly through the guest room's door, he finds me still awake. He pulls back the covers, and I move over, expecting that he will lie beside me, hold me in apology for the words of the stepfather I know he dislikes. Imagining his shame, I feel sorry for him. But my father doesn't lie down.
>
> Instead, he lifts up the hem of my nightgown. He doesn't speak, and neither do I. Nor do I make any attempt to stay his hands. Beneath the nightgown I am wearing no underpants, and he opens my legs and puts his tongue between them.
>
> *His mother's house His mother's house* I think the words over and over, aware that such a setting for his advance cannot be insignificant, but not understanding its meaning.
>
> What he does feels neither good nor bad. It effects so complete a separation between mind and body that I don't know what to feel. Across this divide, deep and unbridgeable, my body responds independently from my mind. My heart, somewhere between them, quickens.

> Neither of us speaks, not even one word. The scene is as silent, as dark and dreamlike as if it proceeded from a fever or a drug.
>
> *His mother's house.*
>
> He needs to do it at *his mother's house.* He needs the power granted by her presence, and he needs to thwart that power. (pp. 127-28)

This intricate scene follows an awkward dinner that Kathryn and her father have shared with his mother and stepfather. During lapses in the father's conversation, his stepfather tells obscene racist jokes, while his mother barely speaks. The obsessively repeated and italicized *his mother's house* implies that, just as Kathryn's mother is somehow to blame for the incest, the father's relationship with his mother is also an attribute. The silence between daughter and father draws attention to the unspeakability of their actions and the sense of otherworldliness, of the uncanny, is a constant in the narrative. That Kathryn welcomes him into her bed is, in itself, an unusual gesture between a parent and adult child. The long nightgown seems to mock Victorian sensibilities as her father lifts it, shockingly trespassing on a place fathers should never venture (compare this with the negligée Anaïs is wearing on her first sexual encounter with her father in the hotel at Chamonix, *Incest* p. 207). The fact that Kathryn is not wearing any underpants suggests some kind of insidious availability on her part. If the themes of hunger and appetite permeate the memoir, the act of cunnilingus repeats the father's desire to consume his daughter during that first kiss, but also her desire to be consumed. Kathryn remarks: "[the kiss is] the drug my father administers in order that he might consume me. That I might desire to be consumed" (p. 70). While the motifs of consumption and cannibalism are common in many sexual practices, they take on a greater resonance when it comes to incest; added to this is the undercurrent of vampirism as the father feeds off his own flesh and blood.

Harrison is careful to include the notion of the unbridgeable mind-body split, a motif that is prominent in incest-survivor narratives, and she also interposes "heart" between body and mind. Yet, the almost throwaway phrase—"the body responds"—is unsettling. Is this a confession of orgasm, as unspoken as the word "incest" is throughout the narrative?[9] If so, it is the absolute opposite of Anaïs's refusal to orgasm in Nin's narrative (*Incest*, p. 211). Of course, a bodily reaction to sexual stimuli does not in itself make Kathryn culpable in the incest-act in the way that Anaïs is: people experience physiological responses even if they are unwilling participants in sexual encounters. But this and other references to Kathryn's sexual responses and involvement do suggest a more complicated reading of the daughter-father liaison. Indeed, there are moments in *The Kiss* when the incest-act seems more reciprocal: "At the motel [...] I let my father kiss me the way he wants to, and I kiss him back" (pp. 123-24).

As with Anaïs, Kathryn's fascination with her father begins to wane as she travels through his family territory; she becomes more repelled, if still resigned. "The heat of our kisses was lost long ago on the highways; the weight of him has smothered the passion I once felt; and the workaday drudgery of our contact flattens me to the point that each time I am more still, more silent, more lifeless" (p. 166). Her father remarks: "If it's the sex, we don't have to do it. It's just a means of expressing our commitment to each other. If it's not good for you, we'll find another way" (p. 186). This is a key moment in the narrative and yet very casually inserted by Harrison because it seems to be Kathryn who needs the relationship, as though there is no other way for them to relate to each other: "what could serve both our needs so well as this compulsive, joyless coupling, the use of our bodies to express our desires." In this sense, both their desires are at stake. It seems that neither of them particularly enjoys the sexual monotony, but are nonetheless accomplices in their revenge against the mother.

There is another aspect to their incestuous coupling that links Kathryn's rite of incest to the twinned ideas of pollution and absolution that I explored in my article on Nin's father-romance. Kathryn makes much of the impact of religion on her life. Indeed, the scene described above, where her father finally asks her for what she had dreaded for months, is embedded in a chapter devoted to the theme of religion and how large God looms in her psyche (p. 162). Offering herself up as a martyr for incest, Kathryn states

> I concentrate on mortification of the flesh. I tell myself that if I give myself over to him to be sullied, then by the topsy-turvy Christian logic that exults the reviled, I'll be made clean. I will if I can just do it willingly, trusting in the ultimate goodness of God, and the way in which he sometimes takes unexpected and even repugnant forms, like beggars and lepers, like Saint Dympna's father. (pp. 165-66)

Aligning herself with St. Dympna, Kathryn puts her body through the usual degradation traditionally associated with hagiographical martyrdom, but which today is associated with the traumatized—anorexia, self-cutting and insomnia. As I mentioned earlier, her clothing matches the drab garb of the penitent yet, and wondrously, she keeps her golden hair, a folkloric motif that will finally give her bargaining power.

Kathryn's voluntary outcast state and self-sacrifice to the father, however, is a far cry from Dympna's defense of her body against the lustful advances of a pagan father, and her enforced exiled and subsequent beheading. It seems to me that Kathryn mistakes masochism for martyrdom; the whole point about Dympna's sainthood is that she resists her father at all costs, thus ensuring her integrity. If Dympna's virtue remains intact, Kathryn's is in tatters as she gives herself to her earthly father, convincing herself that the incest-act is in fact an act of absolution. Recalling that incestuous kiss, Kathryn understands it

> not as what he did but as what happened. I've separated him from the act; I've made the adjustment of regarding the kiss as I would a more helpless physical transport, a seizure perhaps, or a spasm of coughing. If the kiss was an accident, outside of human control, then it doesn't pollute the love he has for me. (p. 86)

Yet she knows that she is already infected with the polluting properties of incest and she becomes abject in the way of a traditional pharmakon, carrying the guilt of family secrets on her skin, just as Anaïs becomes the vector for her own and her father's incestuous transgressions. Lying with the father in sordid hotels, which have "rooms for addicts and prostitutes, people who exist outside the social contract" (p. 160), becomes Kathryn's penance. Actually, her father-romance is a *nostalgie de la boue*, a desire for degradation and depravity: for a while she lives "in an underground basement [...] bathed in this dim light" (pp. 115-16). Any attempt to escape such [de]basements results in outbursts of her father's jealousy. Significantly, while in the Dympna legend the father is a pagan-king and the daughter is the converted Christian, in *The Kiss* it is the father who is a "man of God," and who, in fact, authenticates their sexual relationship through the heavenly Father: "'God gave you to me,' he says" (p. 108). In other words, the father's sexual rights are buoyed by God himself: "God announced to my father that He was revealing Himself to my father through me" (p. 113).

Yet, if her father is paralleled with the incestuous father of Dympna, there is also a sense of collusion as Kathryn remarks, "How could she have been martyred without him? How could she have been glorified?" (p. 166). In aligning herself with the patron saint of the sexually abused, how accountable is Kathryn for their incestuous affair? If Kathryn portrays herself as a saint, she is also a "fallen woman," a paradox that informs Nin's portrayal of Anaïs as both angel and whore. Late in the narrative Kathryn asks, "Is there a way to tell a stranger that once upon a time I fell from grace? I was lost so deeply in the wood that I'm afraid I'll never be safe again" (p. 174). "Once upon a time" is a stock phrase for the opening of folk- (and other types of) tales; to be "lost in the woods" is to have lost one's path which, taken allegorically, means to wander into error or sin. Kathryn and her father travel to Muir Woods in northern California. It is "so shrouded in blue fog that the road is [as] lost" as the daughter. To her maternal family, she becomes "the lost child, the child snatched away by the lost father" (p. 176).

Kathryn's father-romance is a journey through the sites of nature's traumas—the Petrified Forest, Monument Valley and the Grand Canyon—unreal locations in the book, uncanny "nowheres and no-times [that] are the only home we have" (p. 4). These ancient, unforgiving places are also psychic landscapes, mythic as much as they are natural habitats that do not seem so incongruous a location for a rite of incest. Kathryn's journey is one of geographical estrangement, a liminal space that the illicit couple seems to pollute as they journey through the world of the *unspeakable*. After the initial "honeymoon" period, their love becomes as barren as the deserts they drive through, and subject to the same undercurrents of separation and displacement. Harrison traces a journey back to origins as a means of describing the loss the daughter (and father) have suffered. Both are looking for this lost something in each other and in the landscape around them, while deliberately occluding the object of their original (be)longing and the thing that binds them, the mother. Ultimately, what has been outlawed is the possibility of Kathryn's position as her father's proper daughter; her transgression has taken her beyond that once sought-after role and now her status is unspeakable. "We lost each other. We lost my childhood and his fatherhood and twenty years of love, and these losses are not recoverable. We are fleeing from this truth, but we can't flee indefinitely" (pp. 106-107).

If Kathryn falls into a type of paralysis as a response to her father's inappropriate kiss, it is the goodbye kiss she gives her grandfather as he lies in his coffin that ignites her slow awakening:

> [t]he kiss I place on [my grandfather's] unyielding cheek begins to wake me, just as my father's in the airport put me to sleep. I am transformed from a person who assumed she had time to squander to one who knows that no matter how many years her fate holds, there will not be enough. (p. 190)

What does not become apparent to the daughter until it is too late is that there was always a father figure present in her life. Yet this is not the final grand gesture of Kathryn's rite of incest. It is when her mother lies on her death-bed at the age of forty-two that the daughter makes the mythic gesture of offering up her golden hair to show that the affair with her father is finally over. "In the hospital, I lay the severed ponytail, twenty-three inches long, on her bed" (p. 195). In chopping off her "princess hair"—an act of extreme penitence—Kathryn is seeking absolution from the mother while simultaneously severing herself from her father, whose admiration for her hair is made evident from the beginning of their relationship.[10] When he discovers what she has done, "he grieves [...] as he does not over my telling him I've been accepted in graduate school, that I'll be moving away in the next few months. "'How could you take it [the hair] from me!' he cries" (p. 197). With the death of her mother, and in terms that resonate with Nin's resolution of her own rite of incest, Kathryn's father-romance ends as it begins, with estrangement.

The loss of my father will haunt me as it did in the days long past, when I saw a man with no face walk the halls in our house. Somewhere in the world there is a father I can't know. Once he was unknown in his absence, and now that I have known him, and he me, the rest of my life depends on our exile from each other. (p. 202) ❖

Works cited

Girard, René. *Deceit, Desire and the Novel.* [*Mensonge romantique et vérité Romanesque*, 1961]. Tr. Yvonne Freccero. Baltimore and London: The Johns Hopkins University Press, 1965.

Harrison, Kathryn. *Thicker Than Water.* New York: Avon Books, 1992.

----. *The Mother Knot.* New York: Random House, 2004.

----. *The Kiss.* New York: Random House, 2011 [1997].

Nin, Anaïs. *In Favour of the Sensitive Man and Other Essays.* London: W.H. Allen & Co, 1981.

----. *Winter of Artifice.* London: Peter Owen, 1991.

----. *Incest.* San Diego; London; New York: A Harvest Book, Harcourt, 1992.

Owen, Jean. "Interview with Kathryn Harrison." Jan, 2013, unpub.

Notes

1 Kathryn Harrison is one of New York's most prolific and perplexing writers. To date she has published seven novels: *Thicker Than Water* (1992); *Exposure* (1993); *Poison* (1995); *The Binding Chair* (2000); *The Seal Wife* (2002); *Envy* (2005); and *Enchantment* (2012); two memoirs: *The Kiss* (1997) and *The Mother Knot* (2004); two collection of essays, *Seeking Rapture: Scenes from a Woman's Life* (2003) and *True Crimes* (2016); one travel memoir, *The Road to Santiago* (2003); and three 'real life' studies: *Saint Thérèse of Lisieux* (2003), *While They Slept: An Inquiry into the Murder of a Family* (2009), and *Joan of Arc* (2014).

2 For a full account of Nin's father-romance, see my article "Anaïs Nin's Father Romance as a rite of incest" in *A Café in Space: The Anaïs Nin Literary Journal* (Vol. 14, 2016, pp. 39-51).

3 I interviewed Kathryn Harrison via email while researching my PhD thesis, "Narratives of Daughter-Father Incest: Ovid's Myrrha, Anaïs Nin and Kathryn" (Jan. 2013). A full transcript can be found in Appendix 1 of the thesis. In the article, quotations from the interview will be indicated thus: (Owen/Harrison Interview).

4 In *In Favour of the Sensitive Man*, for instance, Nin writes: "I continued to be dependent on the therapist ever so many years because he delivered me from cultural guilt and projected me into new cycles. Each cycle was a different drama. The first one was the relation with the missing father, the second cycle was the relation to the mother from whom I took the concept of female sacrifice, the third was the creation of my own creative will. A final, synthesizing analysis by a woman finally brought me to a harmony among all the other parts of myself" (p. 63).

5 That their accounts of incest were published at the height of the confessional era is of significance too, especially as they were met with a similar reception in that the opinions of critics were divided between those who are scandalized and those who celebrate these confessions. Adult-centered incest narratives are ambiguous; coercion and complicity come together at an incestuous impasse; but it is this that makes Nin and Harrison unusual, riveting and useful in the history of woman-authored and daughter-led narratives.

6 This model of triangular desire has been theorized by René Girard as "mimetic" whereby, rather than coveting an object on its own merits, the subject mimics the desire of someone she or he has taken as a model or mediator. Girard argues that such triangularity falls into two categories: the first type is "'external mediation,' in which a distance is established

between the "subject" who desires and the model of that desire. The second category is "internal mediation," which involves a model that is not distanced from the subject and thus more readily becomes a rival and obstacle in the subject's quest for the object. It is internal mediation and an oedipal formation that underpin Kathryn's rite of incest.

7 The mother-daughter relationship in this and a follow-up memoir *The Mother Knot* (2004) is of significant interest in its own right but is, unfortunately, outside the scope of this article.

8 I do not have space in this article to examine the father's incest trajectory. Suffice to say, he is unable to let go of the image of his teenage wife, and so he uses his daughter as a substitute. He is able to re-enact his adolescent love affair, but this time he can alter the original ending by running away with his daughter.

9 Actually, Harrison refers to the daughter father relationship as an "affair"—see, for instance, pp. 78, 160—which is more akin to the language of adultery. This is a stark contrast to Nin's blunt title *Incest*.

10 Kathryn's fairy-tale hair (she likens herself to Rapunzel) is "a symbol of *me*, of how I differ from my mother: long versus short, blonde versus brunette" (p. 194). When she visits Gheel in Belgium, years later, Kathryn remarks on the uncanny likeness her hair bears to that of the statue of Dympna sculpted by Jan van Wavre (in the early sixteenth century): "[Dympna's] father cuts off her hair, a long blond tail of it, as much like my own as a statue's could be. Except that I don't let my father have that hair, or my life" (p. 196).

Eduardo Sánchez, Joaquín Nin-Culmell, Anaïs Nin

The Problem of Family in *The Diary of Anaïs Nin*

By 1964, Anaïs Nin had, finally, after decades of indecision, a plan to release her long-awaited diary in a way that those she wrote about would not be harmed. As we now know, the first volume of the Diary covers the years 1931-1934, the time during which Nin met Henry Miller and his wife June and became intimately entangled with both; she also had affairs with both of her psychoanalysts, René Allendy and Otto Rank, as well as an incestuous relationship with her father, Joaquín Nin. All of this was unbeknownst to her husband, Hugh (Hugo) Guiler, who was still alive during the diary's publication. In order to keep these secrets, she excised her entire sensual life from the published diary and only included what some may consider "hints" at intimacy.

Guiler, a banker who was careful to keep himself out of the limelight (and who had a fear of being labeled a bohemian), opted out of the diary entirely. The only mention of him, and not by name, is in Nin's agent/co-editor Gunther Stuhlmann's introduction. But there were others who needed protection, and they included Nin's brother, Joaquín Nin-Culmell who was the chairman of UC Berkeley's music department, and her cousin, Eduardo Sánchez.

Of the two relatives, Nin-Culmell was by far the most cooperative, even going as far as helping Nin with factual information about the family and events. Sánchez was another story—although he and Nin had been very close in their younger years and even had a dash of romance in their relationship, he was a closet homosexual and was terrified of exposure. This led to a rather bitter exchange between the two as Nin felt he was a very important character during the early 1930s and wanted to include him in the diary, while he pushed back vehemently.

A side note: in 1965, Letters to Anaïs Nin *by Henry Miller was published by Putnam, which, because Miller was notoriously famous at the time, caused quite a stir in the literary world. Miller, as a way of paying Nin back for decades of financial support, gave her the entirety of the royalties.*

The following letters come from a batch of correspondence in folders organized by Nin's literary executor and lover, Rupert Pole, which are simply labeled "1964" and "1965."

Letter from Anaïs Nin to Eduardo Sánchez:

Los Angeles, May 26, 1964

Dear Cousin: Can't understand what happened to your letter. Did you write to 9 Washington Square Village, New York City 12? Could it be that Millicent forwarded it to the Crillon where we did not stay? And worse still, you do not seem to have received two letters I wrote you, one long one about work on diary, your part in it, horoscopes, etc., and another about going to

Paris and whether I would see you (May 1 to May 20). The important thing as that you are invited to stay with us. You can have my room and private shower. Both Hugo and I will be very glad to have you. At least if you have this you can take your time to look around for a cubby hole as I know you like your privacy. But you are warmly welcome. Let Hugo know. I wrote you because my horoscope seems to have taken a turn for the best; rather late. Marguerite Duras loves my books, accepted to do screenplay for *A Spy in the House of Love*, my agent became a producer and sold the idea to Robert Wise. Hard to believe, eh? It's done. In Paris I was received like a celebrity, interviewed every day, on television, on radio, met a horde of friends, readers, young writers, and had a 20-day euphoria to feel "connected" again with the people I love. Me and all the critics. I am now in Los Angeles basking in publicity, trying to work quietly, while Duras works on script, Wise visits her in the middle of June. It cheered Hugo. I was able to help him this very difficult year for him with $6,000 I received for Miller's letters to me to come out in Putnam's edition in the fall. Miller gave me that for having helped him in the past.

Film won't be made until February.

I hope this letter reaches you.

Welcome to Washington Square Village. Your beautiful desk will also be glad to see you again.

Love,

Anaïs

Later in 1964, Sánchez left for Florence, Italy, where he was doing research.

Letter from Eduardo Sánchez to Anaïs Nin:

Florence, October 25, 1964

Dear Anaïs: Sorry, but at the moment I find that we are out of step, and I only hope it won't last too long. But don't exaggerate the details. When I arrived in New York on June 7, I called your apartment on two different mornings, but there was no answer, not even from Millicent, so I decided Hugo was away and you were in California—and I waited. Fortunately, you found out where I was staying.

It would be impossible to explain in a letter the negative mood I am in, and have been in for the past year, ever since I came face to face with old age and death, and the shock has been so terrible that I have not been able to react except negatively. I have become a stark existentialist. Life is absurd.

However, I am not completely negative and insensitive. My pity and sympathy can be aroused, and they are being aroused by my friends. And so when I found out that you and Hugo were doing so beautifully physically, spiritually and socially, I realized you didn't *need* me. But my friends did.

So, being in the negative state of mind, and not wanting even "immortality" or notoriety, and therefore, wishing to be forgotten, the thought of your publishing part of your diary (the years 1931 to 1935 no less!) depresses me considerably. And I don't see how a discussion over it would be of any help. But don't mind me. You just go ahead. Don't tell me about it, and don't send me a copy. Just remember that the less you say about me the better—that is, while I am still alive. OK? And when you really *need* me, let me know.

Love, Eduardo

On October 30, 1964, Anaïs Nin writes to Gunther Stuhlmann: Please tell me where they are, copies of the *Diary*, as I feel I have to show one to Henry, one to Eduardo, etc.

Letter from Eduardo Sánchez to Anaïs Nin:

Florence, November 8, 1964

Anaïs, for goodness' sake don't spend eighty dollars for a copy of your diary for me. Now that I've read your letter it seems to me there is no need for you to send me a copy. All I ask is that is if it is humanly and artistically possible for you to leave out my personal life, and to tone down as much as possible my homosexual relationships. Is that too much to ask? While I am still alive I do mind very much this display of my miseries.

My plans are to stay here for another year at least—the archives and my research are the necessary drugs which I need acutely at this stage of my life. Of course, and if I can afford it, I shall visit the States next year.

The weather has been just terrible. This winter may be the worst yet, and so I am trying to make my apartment as cozy as possible. Hope to do some writing when I finish my researches on Machiavelli this autumn.

My life here is so peaceful, so uneventful, so routine, I have very little news. For the first time in years I've bought a book on contemporary life: the autobiography of Jean-Paul Sartre. Since his Existentialism is the only honest "philosophy" I've yet found, I was interested in his autobiography. When I finish it I shall send it to you.

Love, Eduardo

Letter from Eduardo Sánchez to Anaïs Nin:

Florence, January 2, 1965

Dear Anaïs:

Please try not to take my irritations too seriously, because my irritations are the result of precocious old age!

Have sent you Sartre's "Les Mots" by airmail to New York. I couldn't finish it, possibly because I am no longer in touch with the 20th century. And let me hasten to confess that I only know of Sartre's philosophy by hearsay, and that because he seems to have more intellectual courage than the religious existentialists, I prefer him. Nevertheless I don't follow him in his corollary: that since there is not life after death, no God, etc., one must combat the absurdity of life by becoming "engaged," joining the communist movement and helping the human species (which is the only entity which seems to have a relative immortality). I only want to "cultivate my garden" as Voltaire suggested.

As for surrealism, it's all right for adolescence, youth, maturity, but not for old age. However, there is really no excuse for discussing this any further. It is just that I thought you would be interested in knowing that I once some months ago saw old age and Death stark naked, and now I am trying to adjust to that formidable experience.

I cannot come to the States every year. Too expensive. We'll see. Anyway, I no longer have citizenship problem. The Supreme Court of USA has ruled that a naturalized American citizen can stay away from the States as long as he pleases. However, I haven't yet made up my mind to stay on in Italy. (And I haven't yet heard of New York University is sending me any pupils as yet!)

As for your dairy I still insist that you do not hurt me by exposing my homosexuality. You haven't yet answered me on that point. Besides, I don't see why you cannot cut me out completely. Certainly the diary will not lose importance, since I am not Henry Miller, Artaud, Allendy, Moricand, etc., etc. Am I really asking too much?

Cariños, Eduardo

Letter from Eduardo Sánchez to Anaïs Nin:

Florence, January 11, 1965

My dear Anaïs:

You finally answered that you were not going to expose my homosexuality, but I don't see how you are going to do it. I have reasons for mistrusting you since you once told my sister and Mama and then later you and Hugo told Puffy Archibald! But honestly now that my blood has chilled completely, I cannot for the life of me comprehend how I could have been homosexual. What an *idiot* I've been the best part of my life! What's worse this is only an acute stubbornness against publicity. My most profound mulishness is being dead-set against any publicity whatsoever. My poor Anaïs, who would have thought that your loving cousin would in the end let you down! Somehow even writing under a pseudonym seems to be a poor subterfuge. I used to amuse myself by calling this singular complex the "Greta Garbo Complex," in other words an unmeasurable desire for fame accompanied by a horror of being *known personally* (this is while I was an actor).

At this moment because I am being a scholar and consequently impersonal. I am doing my damnedest to break through this complex by forcing myself to publish a document I've just discovered (I am trying to be very clever, cornering myself in such a way that I should have to go through with it—for instance, I've already written to an editor. If he says yes, I must perforce finish the introduction I've already half-finished!)

Rereading your letter again, I find that it is only fair that I read your diary before I make up my mind to ask you to cut me out altogether (the solution of changing names I do not accept).

Love, Eduardo

Letter from Joaquín Nin-Culmell to Anaïs Nin:

Oakland, January 21, 1965

Dear Anaïs,

So terribly sorry that I have taken so long in answering your first card, you shorter second card, and to let you know that the diary arrived safely upon my return from New York. Don't worry one bit about the letter. I *would* like to make some helpful (I hope) comments—largely factual—but I simply cannot do it in a rush. Am up to my ears in work and have barely time to keep up with my inescapable work at the university. On the other hand, I realize that Eduardo wants to get at it right away and may have more time than I do at the present time. What should we do? I could send it *without comments* to Eduardo and then have him send it to you to return to me... I do need time and plenty of it even if I do it a hundred or so pages at a time. As you

Joaquín Nin-Culmell, 1930s

know, I read quickly but writing comments takes time and thought. Also, I do not want you to feel censored in any way. I have absolute confidence in your fairness, veracity and appreciation. Let me try and find the time during the next few weeks and if I can get some of it done then it might be easier all around. Too bad Eduardo is such a worry-wart. If I find that I cannot do justice to the problem I will let you know.

Letter from Anaïs Nin to Joaquín Nin-Culmell:

Los Angeles, January 25, 1965

Dear Cuchi: I do understand now much work you have, and how this is a matter which cannot be hurried. Why don't we let it so until the summer when you have time? It is a good project for then. Unless the publisher says suddenly he will take it, and then you can concentrate on it? Is there any way you can have it xeroxed at the college? I mean a do-it-yourself one. They seem to have those machines everywhere. You could have a copy made. Or else, send it to me (it is best to send it in a big manila envelope, a hundred pages at a time, easier, you don't have to go to the post office. I will send then to you all set for mailing. I have calmed Eduardo's fears, promising nothing would be printed without his OK, so that is not the problem so much as to keep it going so I have it ready when the time comes.

The real problem of diary of course is that portraits are necessarily unbalanced (such as the time when Mother was a marvelous mother, the time when I was devoted, and in the diaries I was working on the other day I expressed the love—when you were both in Mallorca and in danger—so one has to read the whole damned thing for symmetry and justice).

Despite Nin-Culmell's hectic schedule, he was able to read the diary and to make comments.

Letter from Joaquín Nin-Culmell to Anaïs Nin:

Oakland, February 1, 1965

Dear Anaïs, Delighted with your letter of January 25th. Quite understand about what you call "unbalanced" portraits. Don't worry about them or my reactions. Don't forget that I too have my own "unbalanced" portraits and that even after all these years they seem to have remained more or less unchanged. What curious animals we are! I love the flow of your writing! Some people have photographic memories. Yours is more like an X-ray and a bit of radar thrown in for good measure! And. yet so tender! How do you do it?

And now back to the diary.

p. 143 Did I mention "I am embalmed" for "*je suis embaumée*"? I loved June's remark about your being born knowing. Can't remember the page.

p. 351 Loulou rather than Lulu?

p. 370 Grandfather Joaquín was not a military man although he disciplined the hell out of Father.

p. 382 Are you sure of the fact that "Les Ruines" was built for d'Annunzio?

p. 383 What about removing the identifiable facts such as "rich Cuban family," "Romeo and Juliet," etc. I don't doubt your memory but I do question the need for these sudden changes into biographical data. Your diary is not that kind of a book and "low flying" should be avoided.

p. 400 Your note unnecessary. I would not identify Gustavo.

p. 404 Ferveur and not fervor.

p. 408 Repeat of things said before. Can't find place.

p. 413 Zadkine. Better said before on p. 376.

p. 420 Father copied d'Annuzio as he copied Manen and others but I doubt very much they shared anything or anybody. The novel where the description of Mother's singing: "*O cessatti di piagarmi*" is to be found in "Nocturne." The story was about your little brother (that's what made it so typically d'Annunzio): "*Tu as les yeux d'un passioné! Gare aux femmes!*"

p. 439 Marguerite. Better said before on p. 435 and before

p. 439 Bushman episode necessary?

p. 442 Same remark as for p. 439 (Marguerite)

p. 452 Father's grandfather was not a teacher. He was an army man, probably a general. Father's father was a teacher and not an army man. He ran a tutorial school of some kind but don't forget his lack of success and Father's need to enlarge reality.

p. 457 Louise's Mother. Better said in section on Louise.

p. 274 The scar business is repeated on p. 429.

p. 464 The car was an American car which, in itself, was a de luxe item but it was not a de luxe American car. Difference?

p. 488 Seduced maid (?¿?) already mentioned in connection with walks along the railroad tracks in Louveciennes.

We did not go to Cuba for Papa To's illness and death. Mother went alone (see train incident).

No trios with Casals. With the Cassado brothers. Where did you pick up the Manen and lsaye business? A trio would not have *two* violinists... What we did hear in Arcachon was the rehearsing of the concerts given in Arcachon (old Italian masters sung by Mother and played by Father)...

p. 489½ D'Annuzio already described. Idem for "Les Ruines."

p. 490 I remember the caterpillars! The cat business (with a cane!) was something else again...

p. 491 Can't understand the "meaning" of men spitting on their hands waiting for the elevator (train?). Cold?

Letter from Anaïs Nin to Joaquín Nin-Culmell:

Los Angeles, February 1, 1965

Dear Cuchi: Your letter delighted me. It was wise, witty and warm. My three favorite qualities. Your comments are very helpful, and I will take note of them. I read your letter to Rupert [Pole] and he was enchanted with my "little" brother suddenly appearing to him in his true grown up qualities. It is true that you have grown up, by golly, and to what insights. I was very proud of your praise, and will answer every point, when I get to work on revisions.

On real story of concert, I think I should tell the *real* version. After all, I had to make a few changes in diary anyway, and this one is important to you and to me.

About history of family, I may, since it is Father who tells it, suggest it was his version, the "legend," etc., not because I care one way or another, but *his* need of this is part of his problem. I stated it as a fact, but all I need to say is that he stated it. It goes well with his need of bolstering by superficial things.

The rest as I go along. But your care and comments are invaluable and interesting in themselves. Very tolerant, very wise. In a way, I am glad this proved and confirmed all you accords, which I thought were merely emotional. *Un vrai frère, quoi, ça ne se trouve pas tous les jours. Je suis e n c h a n t é…*

Letter from Anaïs Nin to Eduardo Sánchez:

Los Angeles, February 1, 1965

Cher cousin: Since you have my promise that not a word will published concerning you, let us study this problem with detachment and calm. I am sending you the pages as they are now (subject to revisions). Joaquín made his helpful revisions, comments, etc. A charming, very mature letter, concerned only with mis-facts. Now. I can take you out altogether which would be a shame for you contributed to the mental climate, books, knowledge and ideas of the group. (Also occasionally I slipped you in instead of Hugo where an objective scene took place.) In any case, remember, the name will be changed. I can remove all clues to your identity so that if any of the family will read it (which I doubt, as none of them read anything at all). I can leave you as a friend, influence, and mentor, which you were, leave you wherever you wish, as a part of talks, games, charades, etc. Now I beg of you, read quietly, gently, and without anxiety. Whatever troubles you, displeases you make note of it. Page so and so. Comment.

For example, Joaquín had a totally different version of what happened at his concert, and I rectified that. Do not feel exposed. You won't be. I was going to precede each section with a physical description of character: you as a handsomer Jouvet. There are beautiful things that are a shame to lose, as in the Proustian sense. For example, my bearing the name of your mother and sister, and therefore symbolically explaining the taboo, are hard for a poet to sacrifice. I could stress one element, and efface another. The romantic brother and sister attachment and our influence on each other, and you taking me to Allendy. Weigh these things. Try to think of them as Proust. You were important. If I respect the homosexuality completely, do you object to the other things? (Always under another name, of course. The only real names I left are those who wish to be named, such as Miller, and others I will consult with in time, such as Rank's wife and daughter, etc.) Above all, as the new generation says, *keep cool.* Keep your mind alert. Make your comments. If you wish to draw a red pencil through all of your existence, do so (not on the script because each copy costs me so much). By the time you return it Joaquín will have another batch coming. I am up to page 1400... A life's work. Trust me. Weigh things as an artist, as a thinker, as a personality which should not be buried. I have long ago understood that some of us cannot bear to expose one's self, and also to respect the image you have. Others' image of us is never matched to our own. I suffered hell when Fred wrote his obtuse book and distorted every fact. I do not think I distort. I will send you a copy of Joaquín's letter. Send it back to Los Angeles where I do the major part of my work. NY is just hell for work. Here I am at my desk at 8 AM till I drop down with fatigue.

Letter from Joaquín Nin-Culmell to Anaïs Nin:

Oakland, February 4, 1965

Dear Anaïs,

Delighted with your delight and so glad that my comments were helpful. I felt a little bit like Tom Thumb following some giant footsteps but even so I could make an attempt at jumping from one imprint to the other... The fact remains that your writing is extraordinarily fluid and bell-like at the same time. It rings true (regardless of the bookkeeping details which are my specialty) but the sound is never harsh. How you can manage to *see* people as you do and still *love* them is beyond my capacity to understand. You must have a monumental capacity for love. No small wonder that human beings fall short of your expectations. It is God you seek.

You are quite right about father's need for bolstering the surface things. It was his most disarming quality (if you caught on to it) and the most destructive (if your life depended on it). I still feel he was a child in many ways. An adolescent husband and a competitor with his children. He had genuine accomplishments but never quite fulfilled the promise of his talent. Perhaps I should say *talents.* He applied his iron-clad discipline to the wrong things. Having escaped from his father he proceeded to "punish" himself in lieu of his father. And so he never quite escaped from his "guilt" but rather added to it like a little boy who can't keep out of the cookie jar. He was ready to make peace with himself and with religion but it had to be done on his deathbed (!!!) like some bad novel he had read and wanted to act out. I could not prevail upon him to see Padre Rey in Havana. I might add that Padre Rey was ready and willing to see him and was quite a different cup of tea from our dreadful Altermann. He wanted his deathbed scene and he got it! St. Peter must have a special place for children who never grow up.

Letter from Eduardo Sánchez to Anaïs Nin:

Florence, February 7, 1965

Dear Anaïs:

From your last letter I am convinced that you do need me—and want me in your book. All right. Send me a copy, and let's see.

Let me repeat again that now that I am an old man with chilled blood, I look at my homosexual interludes as a series of aberrations ending in miserable failures. I have been a complete and utter idiot! So, the less said about it, the better. Of course, if I am going to remain in your diary, my homosexual tendency must or should be implied. But I will not allow any discussion of my relationship with Féri (was that his name), and his relation to me and to you, and his confessions, and my confessions, etc., etc. "ad nauseum." See?

If only my life could have been on the same level of objectivity, coolness, steady purpose and deep satisfaction I am in now. What satisfaction!

Love, Eduardo

Letter from Eduardo Sánchez to Anaïs Nin:

Florence, March 10, 1965

Dear Anaïs:

Just to let you know that the first part of your manuscript arrived safely, although a little battered.

Naturally I read it immediately in a few hours, and took some notes. I was most favorably impressed. But I promise you that I will be very objective and critical.

I shall reread it more slowly, take down more notes—then compose my first impression with the second. Afterwards I shall try to express my opinions.

So this is only to let you know it has arrived, and that I shall spend more time on it.

Cariños, Eduardo

Letter from Eduardo Sánchez to Anaïs Nin:

Florence, March 23, 1965

Dear Anaïs:

Yesterday I mailed "registered" your manuscript in two packages. It may take five weeks to reach Los Angeles. I do hope they will arrive safely and well. (I still don't understand why you didn't show me the manuscript when I was last in New York, or allow me to take it down to Miami.)

You succeeded so well in eliminating Hugo that I am encouraged to believe that with just a little effort you can erase me completely. Do try again. Please. Besides, I believe you are not exercising your instinct for selectivity. You are bringing forth out of your diary people who should remain there, and not clutter your manuscript. I am a neurotic, negative being, so why bring me in? Why not stick to the famous, the important, the interesting, the creative (you have certainly brought out vividly Allendy, Rank and Miller). And you say I met Artaud? Possibly once, but I can't remember. Rank I'd consulted once. It was unforgettable.

I know you don't want criticism, but just the same I will compare you to people who are color-blind. Anaïs, you are vulgarity-blind, and when you try to be vulgar, or try to imitate Miller, the result is so out of color, so preposterous, so utterly vulgar that instead of shocking, it *dismays*. That description of your and Henry's visit to the whore house is AWFUL!

At one moment, I had thought you had found a brilliant way of showing Henry's vulgarity: by publishing *his own notes*, so that when on page 99 he uses the word "shit," that four-letter word, that strident note was perfect, just the right necessary note to climax Henry's sense of vulgarity. But when you try to describe his vulgarity literally, and on page 103 you give a string of four-lettered words, the result is a vulgarization of vulgarity which is preposterous and pitiful (and while we are on this subject, let me advise that if you use "cunt-writer" once it should be enough).

Now, on a more personal level, I do question your intuitions or your taste at times. You had worried that I wouldn't accept the three Anaïses—conceit. I didn't bat an eyelash. But did you think that your having me, in front of your future public, masturbate as the age of six, would make me chuckle with glee? Anaïs, this is an intimate, psychoanalytical, clinical, professional secret. (Besides, it is only a psychoanalytical Freudian supposition. I only remember the punishment and the guilt etc. Why wouldn't my crime have been that I tried to rape my mother?!)

You seemed to have felt a sense of delicacy in not exposing your father. It's his own type of masturbation (the ripped trouser pockets—and his manipulating girl-pupils while at the piano). He is dead now, and wouldn't mind. I am alive, and wouldn't mind? As though you had me already dead! I was doing so well in your manuscript, quiet, silent, in the background, mysterious, coming forward now and again, to take Hugo's place, or someone else's, saying just a phrase, or just a sentence, not important, just to keep myself alive until—bango!—I masturbate at the age of six, or, what is silly and even the epitome of banality, until you have me say (page 131): "I have a feeling I am coming to my mother..." etc.

No, my dear Anaïs. I shall be 61 next month. Please try the impossible: be realistic. I cannot change my negative pattern. I did not change when I was young. I cannot change now.

I am so sorry, so terribly sorry.
Eduardo

On March 26, 1965, Anaïs Nin writes to Hugh Guiler: Eduardo's reaction to *Diary* absolutely irrational, personal and highly distorted. But I promised to leave him out altogether.

On March 26, 1965, Anaïs Nin writes to Gunther Stuhlmann: Eduardo has been the only neurotic who wants every mention out. He wants to remain the invisible man. But he is not an important element. His obsession is secrecy.

Letter from Eduardo Sánchez to Anaïs Nin:

Florence, April 2, 1965

Dear Anaïs,

I am so grateful that I am being left out—a million thanks (just a most inadequate expression for expressing the inexpressible).

Good luck, my dear, as ever, your cousin Eduardo

On April 9, 1965, Anaïs Nin writes to Hugh Guiler: Eduardo says nothing about coming. His request to be completely out of diary is what Joaquín aptly describes as a strange way to commit suicide. All he had, after reading 815 pages, was a violent reaction to a ten line episode on masturbation, which was going to come out, as per our agreement, and nothing to say about entire DIARY except an outraged criticism of visit to the whore house. My most negative statements about him have been confirmed by time. Negative, neurotic, and petty. Above all, absolutely without sense of history, for I cannot but regard the past as history, no longer personal. Don't you? The real artist has to transpose, he can't live with all that alive-and-kicking in the womb all the time.

On April 18, 1965, Anaïs Nin writes to Hugh Guiler: A summer day. Changed all the names. Eduardo (oh, revenge) has become a girl, Marguerite, Allendy's patient who had the comical episode with him. Unconscious?

On April 23, 1965, Anaïs Nin writes to Hugh Guiler: The avarice of Eduardo is only one manifestation of a much deeper avarice of feeling. I did not write you about his reaction when I sent the diary to him for approval of references to him, offering to take them all out, so he could read without anxiety. He reacted only to the passage of his childhood experience (masturbation) blew up at that, and found absolutely not one word to say about the 815 pages! Attacked the vulgarity of the whorehouse visit. That *was all*! A little grain of sand obscured the whole vision. So I took him out. All I said about his role in our life, initiation to analysis and surrealism, his qualities, was lost on his one neurotic fear of exposure of his sexual life when I had made this a promise. Generosity.

Letter from Anaïs Nin to Joaquín Nin-Culmell:

Los Angeles, April 30, 1965

Dear Cuchi:

You have proved to be the most understanding of all my readers. I am glad we had this opportunity for me to discover your insight, and more of you than I knew from our rare encounters. Your comments deserved careful consideration, so here is a step-by-step response to them as I worked.

Fixed spelling of Banquo

Seduction of the maid was necessary to justify her "revenge," her wanting to kill us (and story I did not tell, that she went after Mother with a big carving knife). How else could one justify her act?

Thanks for catching all the repetitions. I repaired those. Osborne, through a minor character, played an important role, introducing Miller, going mad because of conflict between Montparnasse and his job, and later in the comic incident of Rank wanting to help him and his not believing it was Rank. I have to keep him.

Drake: sometimes a minor character is necessary to show it is a diary as I eliminated so many, to concentrate on the important ones that finally it does not read like a diary at all. Agree? It also shows other side of Montparnasse in which I was not involved.

The difference between notes, mine, Miller, letters and quotations is being taken care of by the typist who is indenting all that is not my writing. A good system.

I had to cut out Eduardo completely according to my promise to let him decide. Sweet revenge, as I had to find someone who initiated me to psychoanalysis, to surrealism, and to be there occasionally at discussions, I turned him into a girl Marguerite... Ha...

I erased identifying references to Duran, Vilmorins, etc.

You are wonderful at catching repetitions. I will ask you to be my number one editor.

Incidentally, two readers have already told me they would have liked to know more about you. An encore...it was out of delicacy that I did not put too much in.

Fixed the Salle Chopin incident.

Fixed matter of mother's age. (If mother was 30 Nin was 22.)

Softened grandmother's lovers. (Mitigating circumstances)

Fixed the injection story. Simply gave permission for calmant injection for pain.

Fixed chronology of trips to Cuba. Confused though, in my mind. As I knew I had been there when I was very small. You mean we all went, saw grandfather, I got Typhoid, Thor was born, we returned to France, and then mother went again alone?

Guell history I left as told by father, not by me.

Fixed embalmed. It was embalmed. I felt stifled with guilt due to my awe of nuns.

LouLou and LuLu, you were right, but changed all of Louises's names, alas, as family is very alive and very prominent.

Yes, Les Ruines was built for D'Annunzio. A few facts like that, remember, were told to me by Father later. He talked a lot then. It was in Paris that he told me the story of his playing with Manen. And playing with Casals (not at the same time, no doubt, so I merely mentioned musicians he had played with, not in quartets). OK?

I removed rich Cuban family Romeo and Juliet.

Fervuer, nor fervor (Artaud)

Thanks for pointing up where I described Zadkine better.

Woman's vanity. I wanted D'Annunzio to notice my eyes. Yours were better. Honest.

Buchman necessary because it points up social consciousness of a special sort. Humanism. As I never joined any political movements I have preserved the idea of individual efforts at rendering justice.

Fixed grandfather and great grandfather mix-up.

Caught repetition of scar section (I want to leave a scar upon the world).

An American car, not De Luxe.

Took out second seduction of maid.

Jews spit in their hands. Took it out.

Explained first quarrel aboard ship between father and mother. Reason for taking us to N.Y. OK. Will fix that. Can't find it but will.

The only thing I can't please you with is removal of the Killgoer episode. It is a comic relief, and Ethel behaved like the woman in the Little Foxes (the classic smile of Bette Davis). I changed the names.

It was not Bachelu father took to Algeria. I met the girl. She was very young, and inexperienced, and I was jealous. Yes, father told me story of Bachelu and Jeanne Gautier on another occasion, how he had to seduce her to prove he could seduce a lesbian.

I made it clear that the house I describe in *Winter of Artifice* and quoted in the diary was father's house in Paris. Did you ever see it?

Yes, you are right, Miller had a great deal to say, but it was not important, and he said a lot, but it had very little depth or meaning.

Fixed Altermann. Who converted Stravinski? Someone did. Your bookkeeping details about which you are so modest, were very helpful.

Yes, a diary records things as said in the heat of the moment, as in the heat of anger, which are out of balance.

Alas, for better or for worse, but I do want to catch the things I didn't mean, or which were said exaggeratedly.

Enormous job of revising. Now I must consider Miller's comments. Complying with small things so he won't get mad at the big ones. Such as that Fred has brains, that *Tropic of Cancer* never had 1000 pages, that he never suffered from not being a handsome man, that June was Romanian and not Hungarian, that he never hated America, etc. *C'est très drôle*, but it is a fact that portrait painters are well acquainted with.

How do you feel about being more present in the diary? You were, of course, in the early ones, in the early Paris period, Rue Schoelcher, in Louveciennes. It was after that really that you were farther away. Traveling, etc. I cut out a lot because it was intimate, and I was always doting on you, and maybe felt you did not want to be featured too much. Think about it. I would like to put things in that do you good as a composer. Help me. You deserve star billing. Only the closer a person is, the more one keeps portrait in a niche marked: not literary.

Letter from Joaquín Nin-Culmell to Anaïs Nin:

Oakland, May 5, 1965

Dear Anaïs,

We must have a special power of transmission for whenever I write to you "out of the blue" a letter from you never fails to materialize the very same day! ¡Olé!

Thank you for your comments about mine and for giving them such careful consideration. I quite agree with all of your changes and, of course, with your conception of the diary being a manner of spiritual thermometer. When the fever goes up, so does the diary! It is all a part of your inner development and as such is of a quality quite extraordinary. Don't worry if I have over-praised you… That is the privilege of a doting brother (and sister!)…

The injection business with regard to Papa struck a sensitive spot with regard to Mother. One more decision she had to make because of the fact that the people who surrounded her were incapable of assuming their responsibilities. Father's comments about this were loaded. Easier to let one's mother die of cancer *at a distance* than to be on the spot and having to make a perfectly moral decision. In any case, all of these decisions were to mark Mother for life and that too is an awesome thing to behold.

When Mother went alone to Cuba, I wasn't born. Papa Thorvald [Culmell] died before 1908. You first went to Cuba when Thorvald was born and then we all returned after I was born. End of collective trips to Cuba.

Be sure to get out from under the Guell business. Family still very prominent in Barcelona (patrons of Gaudi, etc.) and they would have a "fit" with Father's fancies.

I never saw Father's house in Paris but I understand that it was a masterpiece of symmetry. You make it sound more interesting.

Nobody "converted" Stravinski. Nadia Boulanger tried very hard and so did Roland Manuel. For all I know, he is still an Orthodox Russian. Like all men of his generation, he has flirted with Aristotle and Saint Thomas but I fear that it never led him anywhere. Altermann was a friend of Debussy and did write some articles on him before becoming a priest. This aura enabled him to approach intellectuals in general. He now directs a home of oriental students in Paris. Certainly hope he has softened his approach!

With regard to Miller's comments, I would keep a careful note of the changes. Eventually you might entitle the latter "Double Exposure"...

Everything else is OK. Sorry about Eduardo. As for me, the only star billing I want is in your heart. I quite agree with you about portraying people who are close. One of the reasons, perhaps, why I am jumpy about Mother.

Love, Joaquín

Letter from Anaïs Nin to Joaquín Nin-Culmell:

New York, Summer 1965

Dear Cuchi:

Came to N.Y. because Hugo was not recovering from a month-old bronchitis, and he is better now.

Now Darling, I must settle this thing of the relation to the Guells, because entirely aside from the snobbish end, there is a poetic symbolism which I would love to clear up. The Guells are listed as the patrons of Gaudi, the father of surrealism, the first surrealist fantasy architecture. Do you think you might take your courage in your two hands and visit the Guells? Perhaps they might be proud of the distant cousinships, specially if they meet you. Your notes on your inquiries, which I copied from a letter to Thor were equivocal. I am turning in the manuscript in September (signed contract today). I would love to have this clarified. If you have any time in Barcelona it would be an adventure in family history which people would understand. You wrote to Thor that nothing proved it, but nothing disproved it. I would rather think that Joaquín Nin was not a mythomane. Do help me.

My publisher is a darling man, an older scholarly Jew, a writer himself, treats me perfectly, so I permitted many cuts (not vital) to tighten the text. I have already done the next one. Had to take out the Vilmorins, which Americans would not understand anyway...

The Diary of Anaïs Nin, *released on April 15, 1966, was an instant success, erasing decades of struggle and frustration. It propelled Anaïs Nin to a literary superstar status, which she would enjoy until her death in 1977.*

None of the seven volumes of The Diary of Anaïs Nin *mention Eduardo Sánchez by name.* ❖

Hugh Guiler, Eduardo Sánchez, Anaïs Nin, 1930s

Simon Dubois Boucheraud

Anaïs Nin and the Visual Poetry of "Trance Films"

1945-1965

> *I will not just be a tourist in the world of images, just watching images passing by which I cannot live in, make love to, possess as permanent sources of joy and ecstasy (*Fall 1955, *Diary V*, p. 262*)*

Although Anaïs Nin remained devoted, even in the face of the atrocities perpetrated during World War II, to expanding the multivolume diary that was her signal literary achievement, she became increasingly nostalgic about her life in prewar France and more determined than ever to be recognized as a creative artist. By the mid 1940s, she had been laboring for almost two decades with various fiction projects, and had finally published two collections of novellas and short stories, *A Winter of Artifice*, and *Under a Glass Bell*, first in Paris and subsequently in New York, where she undertook the type-setting and printing herself. Most importantly, she had by then published *House of Incest* (1936), and she had completed, in record time, her study of D.H. Lawrence. In those years Nin was straining to break out of the confines of her sheltered life, her early marriage, and the stifling social atmosphere of her husband's business world, all symbolized so perfectly by the heavy iron gate of their rented house in Louveciennes, from where, at times, the luminous city of Paris could be glimpsed in the distance.

The catalysts of her emergence were the then-unknown writer Henry Miller, the gangster-author, and his adventuress of a wife, June. June, the former taxi-dancer, seemed to be the perfect incarnation of a female sexuality Nin herself had never, until then, dared to express or explore except in her imagination. This encounter, and the evolving love affair with Miller, would dominate Nin's emotions for many years to come, but the new life Nin now embraced, within and outside her marriage, became increasingly complex. She found herself involved with the unstable actor-genius Antonin Artaud; with her first analyst, Dr. René Allendy, who was soon to be followed by her second, Dr Otto Rank; and sundry other demanding and draining relationships. Trying to cope with these experiences in her writing, she found the perfect symbol of the self-image that seems to have possessed her at the time, the figure of Alraune, the woman "no man could satisfy."

When she showed Miller the first surrealist pages of the latter manuscript, he was mystified. He asked Nin to explain her "abstractions," which of course were the result of her effort to disguise the true circumstances of her experiences. In her perception, Miller was too sunk in "realism," in trying to probe the mysterious nature of woman in the person of June (whom he called Mona or Mara in his later work) while Nin, in the person of Alraune, presented her own, multi-dimensional image of June as an extension, a missing aspect of her own fragmented selves, as seen under the glass bell of social convention but envisioned in all its poetic distillation.

Highly admiring of the surrealist Dalí-Buñuel film *Un chien andalou* (1928), Nin discussed the use of dreams in writing and was fascinated by the movie, in which "nothing is mentioned or verbalized." Dream material from Nin's original diary was absorbed and transposed into the text of *House*, a practice underlying most of her later fictions.

Praised by Lawrence Durrell as well as by Stuart Gilbert, Henry James's friend and translator, Nin nevertheless feared that she had, in *House*, "carried a fantasy so far that it was inexplicable to others," even though, by 1939, she was able to write: "I recognize the metaphysical authenticity. Writing like *House of Incest* and all the fantasies for which I will not be loved, contains the purest essence of my meaning." She had rebelled against the then prevailing "naturalists," those she termed "reporters of facts," and even against the realism practiced by someone as close to her as Miller.

Nin's husband, Hugh Guiler (aka Ian Hugo), when he tired of the banking world, found his way into filmmaking, and he decided to use the prologue of *House* for his experimental movie "*Bells of Atlantis*." By this time, Nin herself was already engaged in the new medium, since Maya Deren, a pioneer filmmaker and initiator of "visual poetry" and "trance films"—I am using author Amos Vogel's terms here—had made friends with Nin and started using her in her movies.

Maya Deren

Deren's movies had considerable appeal to Nin. Already familiar with psychoanalysis, which she had undertaken and briefly practiced under the aegis of René Allendy and Otto Rank, Nin was fascinated by the unconscious. Persuaded of the validity of Otto Rank's principles, she was particularly sensitive to any theory that considered the artist in all his or her "creative will". For instance, when she attends a conference during which Dalí appears at a lecture in a deep-sea diver's suit, everybody laughs, but Nin, seeking the meaning, notes: "the artist must find his way into the most secret, the deepest and most unconscious self, where lies the real source of creation. Dalí was right, we could even wear miner's suits." In June 1945, after she has seen several of Maya Deren's films, Nin concisely notes in her diary: "truly unconscious dream material, better than the surrealist movies, because no artificial effects" (June 1945). Indeed, Nin did not think much of Surrealism for Surrealism's sake, as she confesses in *Diary VI*:

> So much of the Surrealist art gives the feeling that images did not come from free association or reverie but [were] an intelligent imitation of the

subconscious process. Possibly because when familiar with subconscious associations, one knows there is a pattern and a link. (Winter 1956-57, *D VI*, p. 78)

As the daughter of a Russian Jewish psychiatrist who had emigrated to America in 1922 and sent her to Switzerland for her art studies, Deren shared many of Nin's principles. To describe Deren's films, Nin frequently resorted to the phrase "visual poetry," as a way of providing an intaglio engraving of underground films.

After Nin and Deren met, the latter chose her actors among Nin's group of friends. She summoned them early in the morning—to Central Park, to Wall Street or in her studio—and Nin describes the lack of direction they all felt. Concerning the filming of *Rituals in Transfigured Time*, in 1946, Nin complains:

> She wanted to make improvised films, she expected that, undirected, things would 'happen,' but the era of happenings had not yet developed. When she expected to catch incidentally a scene, a relationship, her amateurs froze. As soon as the camera stopped clicking they resumed the life she had wanted to capture. She did not know how to create the happening. There has to be a suggestion, a theme, as in a charade. (Winter 1963-64, *D VI*, p. 353)

In *Diary IV* (March 1946), Nin explains that there was supposed to be a party scene, and that she and Gore Vidal, among other actors, were trying their best to give the scene a feeling of exchange or vital responsiveness, but that nothing came out. If I were to appropriate one of Tom Stoppard's lines from "Rosencrantz and Guildenstern are Dead," I could say that they "didn't know how to act." It is only when Nin and" the others gave in to their exhaustion that the magic suddenly took over: "When we all became extremely tired, all our 'poses,' our attempts at acting, our self-consciousness disappeared. We let go. And the party Maya wanted materialized. She cheered. Go on, go on, go on. Exhausted, almost on the verge of hysteria, we danced, talked, held hands, or withdrew, or came back, wandered, looked for intimacy. We worked for her for twelve hours" (*D IV*, p. 136). I refer you to the scene in the movie (*Rituals in Transfigured Time*, from 7'00"-8'30").

Like Stan Brakhage, to whom Amos Vogel compares her, Deren banishes all sound from her works, contributing significantly to the "visualization" of new poetic universes, and, paradoxically, eliminating sound in the post-silent film era. Time is reversed, accelerated, slowed, actions are frozen, condensed, repeated or expanded. The haunting and mysterious quality of the visuals, all proceeding in utter silence, make for an abstract rather than narrative structure—as Amos Vogel underscores in *Film as a Subversive Art* (1974).

Nin says she admires Deren's work, but for all her carping about Deren's lack of concern for the actors' efforts, as well as Deren's dismissive attitude regarding symbolism, Nin comments, concerning *Meshes of the Afternoon* (1943) and *At Land* (1944):

> I see the influence of Cocteau, even though her obsession was to employ symbolic acts but to deny that they had symbolic significance. "A flower," she said, "is a flower, a mirror is a mirror, a knife is a knife." But the flower appeared over the vulva, the mirror was covered, and the knife was dug into the table as if thrown by a knife thrower. How could she say there was no symbolic meaning when the woman crawls over a long banquet table? I always felt that it was because her father was a psychiatrist, and that Maya must deny him, his language and his interpretations over and over again. (Winter 1963-64, *D VI*, p. 351)

Nin does not think much of *Rituals in Transfigured Time.* She says Deren overlooks the specific features of each character, and instead of enhancing them, to consider characters as individuals, as Nin says she does in her novel, Deren dehumanizes them, and wants them to act as a group. Nin does not like the interchangeability of personalities that Deren demands (*D IV*, 149). In *D VI*, she notes:

> The quest for ugliness is one I never understood. Was it because Americans were for the most part born in ugliness, familiar with it, and had grown to love it, or because they associated beauty with the undemocratic upper class, art, the past, Europe, and repudiated it? The American definition of realism was ugliness. To avoid being accused of creating illusion, they always showed the same ugly view of everything. Maya magnified the skin blemishes, the knotted nerves, the large ears; she stressed the oily surfaces, the thyroid white of the eyes, the baldness or the pimple. Maya's actors happened to be beautiful. She uglified them. I had never seen as clearly as in Maya, the power to uglify in the eye behind the camera. (Winter 1963-64, *D VI*, p. 353).

When delineating her vision of what she terms "*The Novel of the Future*," Nin relates what lends itself to iconophobia—this fear of the power of visual representation, made in America—to realism in literature. She says:

> The danger of photographic realism is that it discounts all possibility of change, of transformations, and therefore does not show the way out of situations which trap human beings. The reporter who reports a story literally, the documentary which merely informs us of an existing situation are far from the poet-novelist concerned with creating new patterns, discarding the old, finding life inacceptable and seeking to transform it,

> to keep our dynamism alive by breaking down uniformity. (*The Novel of the Future*, p. 199)

Nin stresses the modernist concern, first voiced by Ezra Pound, "Make it new," but her thoughts also mirror Otto Rank's principle that the artist is someone who adjusts the world according to his creative will, rather than the contrary, which would only lead to neurosis.

Finally the last point on which Nin's method of keeping her diary and Deren's art chime is the relation to chronology. If Nin, influenced by psychoanalysis, often emphasizes what she terms "a chronology of emotions," in the discrete though interrelated entries of her diary, Deren similarly comments on her own films:

> Cinema, to be creative, must do more than record. The mechanism behind the lens, like the brain behind the eye, can evaluate the objects before it can decide them attractive or repulsive, casual or surprising. Above all, the analogy must be extended to understand that the strip of film is the memory of the camera. Just as man is not content to merely reconstruct an original chronology, but in his art, conceives new relationships between remembered elements, so the filmmaker can create new realities by the manipulation of the celluloid memories at his disposal. (March 1946, *D IV*, pp. 137-38)

Hugo, and the Barrons

When it comes to her husband's films, which he undertook after he abandoned the business world for those of art and experimental cinema, Nin is sensitive to the same principle, and in her description she stresses free-association:

> We are living the age of the image but this means not only that we can register more perfectly with cameras the external image, but that we can also penetrate and photograph our inner life as if with an undersea camera. In our dreams, and our fantasies, we are all surrealists, impressionists, abstractionists, symbolists. The camera, more exactly than words, is capable of reflecting the inner life and revealing the metamorphosis which takes place between realistic scene and the way our moods color, distort, or alter the scene as through a prism.
>
> The freedom of improvisation expressed in Ian Hugo's films corresponds to our emotional life, which is continuously projecting and retaining on our inner screen previous images. A face we are looking at will suddenly recall another face out of the past by way of a slight resemblance, and the image from the past will blur and interrupt the present face. As James Joyce tried to capture the form of our inner monologues, which accompany but

do not match the flow of our talk, Ian Hugo emphasizes the mixture of dreams, memories, and immediate impressions.

In film, by placing assembling images according to the design of our emotions, we also enter this region below consciousness where experience actually takes place directly as music does, without interference from artificial cerebral patterns. Becoming more and more aware of this inner unconscious life we need a corresponding change in our art forms. (Fall 1953, *D V*, p. 137)

Nin calls for a new object, born out of the cross-fertilization of arts, and the example she cites is, loyally, her husband's *Bells of Atlantis*. She is also convinced that the soundtrack composed by Louis and Bebe Barron, two experimental musicians, is "an electronic score which matches the fluid images and narration. The three elements, sounds, image, and music, fuse" (Fall 1952, *D IV*, p. 98).

In *Bells of Atlantis*, in 1952, Ian Hugo uses footage of the beach, of the ocean's ebb and flow, inspired by the prologue to Nin's *House of Incest*, and the line "I remember my first birth in water." The film evokes the watery depth of the lost continent of Atlantis. It is a lyrical journey into prenatal memory and the theme of birth and rebirth from the sea.

Without the music, the film would not possess the qualities it does. The Barrons make the musical score of *Bells* by activating electronic circuits, to create electronic circuits, which resound idiosyncratically and haphazardly. As the Barrons themselves say, this is not music, but an electronic score, a new artistic tool. They later collaborated with several filmmakers and a new form of art (Spring 1956, *D VI*, pp. 50-52), verging on the psychedelic, was born out of the encounter of words, motion picture and sound.

Kenneth Anger

Under the sign of the psychedelic, Nin's last experience with film took place in 1954, after she first met Kenneth Anger in San Francisco some years before. Anger, then a fledgling artist influenced by Maya Deren, attracted the attention of Cocteau in the 1950s with his movie *Fireworks*. Nin describes Anger a member of the Beat Generation, then in its ascendancy in San Francisco.

Diary V, concerning the fall and winter 1953, recounts a party thrown by two of Nin's friends. The theme was "A masquerade to which we would come dressed as our madness." For example, one of the guests carried two death masks on sticks, one hiding the other, as an illustration of the conflict between sensuality and death. Another had painted his body two colors, white and black, to embody duality (see Fall 1953). Kenneth Anger liked the idea of the party, which lent itself to a dream he had had, and he decided to make a film of it. Each guest was supposed to come dressed in the same costume as for the party. Nin indicates that Anger was working in the same way that Deren did:

He wanted to capture elusive aspects of our personalities, undirected, spontaneous, accidental. [...] The scenes seemed disconnected. There was chaos because the theme was unknown.

Paul said: "In the films Samson is the false man, the man of many faces, that is why he changes costumes all the time. The various women, Renate as sensuous romantic love, Joan as the virgin beauty, Cameron as the satanic woman, and you as the woman of light, all offer him gifts which he rejects. Curtis brings him the wine of ecstasy from the caves of the unconscious. They all drink and are transformed. You, Anaïs, refuse the drink. You have no need of it. You are Astarte, goddess of the moon."

Kenneth Anger asked Renate's son to dip his finger in the goblet, touch his tongue and fall into a deep trance. Renate suddenly felt she did not want to see her child poisoned. For her it was not a symbolic act, but a real danger. No one could convince her that she was confusing symbolism and reality. The reality and the madness mingled and that made chaos and confusion. The links were missing, as in madness. There was a distortion. Love became hatred, ecstasy became a nightmare. Those who began with sensual attraction ended by devouring each other. (December 1953, *D V*, pp. 139-40)

As is obvious in this scene, reality is suddenly preempted by images.

Nothing suggests that Nin was anything but delighted by that scene, but one gets a sense of her reservations regarding Anger's approach when reading her critical essay *The Novel of the Future*, published fourteen years later:

It was psychoanalysis which revealed to me the constant interaction of dream and action. It was a phrase of Jung's which inspired me to write "*House of Incest*." He said: "Proceed from the dream onward." To capture the drama of the unconscious, [She says,] one had to start with a key. A batch of dreams served as a take-off for *House of Incest*. They supplied the atmosphere, its climate, and texture. At the same time, I discovered that the dream had to be expanded, recreated, could not be told literally for then it became flat and one-dimensional as representational realism. One had to find a language for it, a way of describing atmosphere, the colors and textures in which it moved. Henry Miller was writing "Into the Night Life," while I was writing *HI*. The same argument about the difficulties of rendering dream atmosphere came up later when I talked with underground filmmakers, such as Maya Deren or Kenneth Anger. (*The Novel of the Future*, p. 164)

In her tribute to Miller's *Black Spring*, she is particularly sensitive to the aforementioned chapter, and one suddenly has doubts whether Nin is really talking about literature, as if she had found the key for which she calls:

"Into the Night Life" had begun as a parody of *HI* and ended as an experiment of his own, fusing dreams and inventions. The images are incandescent, luminous, transparent. The mystery of dream, its half-born, half-finished images. Miller reshuffled the contents of the physical world, it was a physical image suffused with light, an X ray of our psychic reconstructions, very close to Dalí. (*The Novel of the Future*, p. 180)

In the 1960s, as her novels were gaining more recognition and were translated into French, Nin was introduced to Marguerite Duras through André Bay, her publisher. They were to put their heads together for the filming of *A Spy in the House of Love*, one of Nin's novellas that was rejected by numerous publishers and finally published in 1954. Nin met Duras several times in the cafés of Saint Germain des Près, and Robert Wise (director of *The Sound of Music*, and *West Side Story*), was supposed to carry out the project. However, if Nin was clearly enthused about Duras's "elusive dialogues, indirect approach to situations and extraordinary poetic suggestiveness," (Spring 1964), Wise begged to differ, and begged off the project. Nin surmised that the combination of her misty writing and Duras's oblique style was "bound to produce pure fog." (*D VI*, p. 361).

Conclusion

I am a fervent believer in the enriching influence of one art upon another, a believer in cross-pollination between the arts, which is now expressing itself in the integration of the arts, in the use of lights, sounds, happenings, theater, sculpture on the stage (such as Noguchi's sets for Martha Graham). (*The Novel of the Future*, 1968, p. 164)

Clearly *D V* and *D VI* are the diaries of an intellectual. Both volumes were, of course, highly edited, but Nin was, at the time she is describing, still bitter not to have published her diary. The two volumes are not as enthralling as the previous ones, since in lieu of Nin's personal thoughts and emotional turmoil, the reader is presented with a series of reviews of books, films and plays, interspersed with letters from friends or other artists, and these volumes feature few personal entries—still, curious fingers can find many in the corresponding handwritten diaries held at UCLA. We can all be greatly indebted to Paul Herron for his unrelenting effort. With this new unexpurgated volume *Trapeze*, it now becomes easier to study this period of Anaïs's life in all objectivity.

The most striking event, one that Nin deliberately chose, is the experiment with LSD for which she volunteered. As she had terminated the first volume of her edited diary, published in 1966, with a suspect stillbirth, and ended the two subsequent volumes with, respectively, the outbreak of World War II and the end of it, volume V ends with a description of her experience with LSD under medical supervision, at a time when Huxley had aroused interest in psychedelics with his book *The Doors of Perception*, in which he adumbrates the effects of a drug that induces dreams, fantasies, and hallucinations; discloses aspects of reality not observed before; intensifies vision and observation; and releases the imagination. To account for the Surrealist strokes in her novels, and to tweak an America whose incapacity for abstraction she denounces, Nin humorously wonders whether she should not pack LSD with each of her books, since several friends confess to only having understood the meaning of the novels under LSD.

However the most interesting aspect of these two late volumes of the *Diary* is the vocabulary Nin resorts to. She uses visual images more and more frequently to describe textual substance. For instance, about *Justine*, by Lawrence Durrell, she confides:

> Justine is an exceptional adventure into intimate experience, a love affair with characters rarely encountered in modern fiction and with the sensuous, beautiful city of Alexandria. Justine has the deep warm colors of a Chagall painting. The blending of humor, skillful analysis, poetic descriptions with realism and surrealism gives it a smoky, mysterious, enticing quality of multiple dimensions." (Fall 1957, *D VI*, pp. 109-110)

The same words are used to describe literature and visual arts, since they are all guided by one and the same principle: psychoanalysis and the quest to unravel the threads of the unconscious. But the language pertaining to visual arts also instills itself in the diary, even for mundane concerns, making of Nin the diarist a prose "filmmaker" of a work she often described as a "motion picture of growth." To her last Jungian analyst, she comments:

> I discuss with [my analyst] the unfortunate habit I have of cutting friendships as soon as someone hurts or betrays me. If they damage, disappoint me, I pack off and leave, and this is no solution. Even my novels are full of "cuts." "Cut!" says director Nin, as if it were a film being made [...]. (Fall 1959, *D VI*, p. 203) ❖

Selected filmography

Anger, Kenneth:
Inauguration of the Pleasure Dome (1954)

Deren, Maya:
The Witch's Cradle (1943)
Meshes of the Afternoon (1943)
At Land (1944, 15 min.)
A Study in Choreogaphy for Camera (1945)
Rituals in Transfigured Time (1946)

Hugo, Ian (Hugh Parker Guiler)

Ai-Ye (1950)
Bells of Atlantis (1952)
Jazz of Lights (1954)
Melodic Inversion (1958)
The Gondola Eye (1963-71)
Through the Magiscope (1969)
Apertura (1970)
Aphrodisiac I (1971)
Aphrodisiac II (1972)
Ian Hugo: Engraver and Filmmaker (1972)
Levitation (1972)
Transmigration (1973)
Transcending (1974)
Luminiscence (1977)
Reborn (1979)

Works cited

Nin, Anaïs. *House of Incest* [1936] (Athens: Swallow Press/Ohio University Press, 1998).

----. *The Diary of Anaïs Nin. Volume IV, 1944-1947* (New York: Harcourt Brace Jovanovich, 1971).

----. *The Diary of Anaïs Nin. Volume V, 1947-1955* (New York: Harcourt Brace Jovanovich, 1974).

----. *The Diary of Anaïs Nin, Volume VI, 1955-1966* (New York: Harcourt Brace Jovanovich, 1976).

----. *The Novel of the Future* [1968] (Athens: Swallow Press/Ohio University Press, 1986).

Vogel, Amos. *Film as a Subversive Art* (New York: D.A.P/C.T Editions, 1974).

Jessica Gilbey

Navel-Gazing into the Light

"Anaïs Nin, for instance, is my idea of a navel-gazing, hyper-sexed bore..." (Daphne Merkin in *The New York Times*, June 16, 2002.)

The critique of navel gazing commonly befalls Anaïs Nin in book reviews and biographical descriptions alike. This special brand of nonsense was especially prominent during the notorious smear campaign *The New York Times* inflicted upon Nin in the 1990s before falling silent on her completely and thus effectively silencing much of the surrounding popular discussion of her. We've seen the critique many times over, always praising objectivity and fictional characters as some kind of literary ideal—achievable only by the most elevated authors (psychopaths?) somehow able to remove all connection of their own humanity to their work with clinical deft and mastery. Self-examination is *sometimes* celebrated, but only if conducted by those who are privileged enough to be seen as worthy and legitimate subjects. Disappointingly, the same act by others (who some would deem "nasty women") is not always afforded equal cultural value but dismissed as if it were a boring self-indulgence rather than vital self-expressive, connective, and sustainable transformational practice.

Navel-gazing is a diminutive term often employed to belittle the work of women who explore deeply personal and intimate details of their inner lives, dismissing them for gazing into what Nin called their "*Cities of the Interior*." The accusation is itself myopic and absurd, because it erroneously assumes that self-exploration limits an individual, blinding them to all else, rather than understanding that it is precisely this exercise in self-examination that allows a person to reflect on how they might project their own limitations and bias into the world. This thus allows them to consider how they might alter those interactions if they a produced by psychological distortions or are in other ways unsuitable (potentially then catalyzing great expansion and change at a larger level). Any intentions to better impact our external environment can only be fulfilled if we understand ourselves. These reflections allow for the path to an evolution of the personal that would lead to a shift in consciousness and greater knowledge at all scales. In a self-published piece titled *On Writing*, Nin explained that:

"[T]his personal relationship to all things, which is condemned as subjective, limiting, I found to be the core of individuality, personality, and originality. The idea that subjectivity is an impasse is as false as the idea that objectivity leads to a larger form of life."

The term itself etymologically and biologically relates to our umbilical connection to our past and to our mothers. Ancient Greeks called this act Omphaloskepsis, referring to it as a meditative practice from which to contemplate the world. This closed portal that once served as a vital link between us and our maternal origin also symbolically represents our connection between the inner psychological world and the outer one, as the individuation process separates us from total fusion with our mothers, we then must learn our place as both separate and related beings. The umbilical cord long gone, our navels are a kind of scar, a reminder that we are shaped by this violent separation, but also that we then shape the world that we perceive through our individual experiences. Navels remind us that we are relational human beings, once literally requiring nourishment from another, and simultaneously our separate experiences are not always universal.

This nostalgia of the bodily connection we once had, binding us to another, is the same place from which we can contemplate ourselves and how we then present our realities into the narratives that become our lives. For example, Anaïs Nin's famous quote, prolifically posted and reposted on the internet is "we do not see things as they are, we see them as we are." Sure enough, many of her novellas and her diaries explore this fundamental insight to our psychological influence on our subjective experience. Liberation isn't found by escaping ourselves, but rather by using our lives to understand and recognize other individuals and their experiences in comparison and contrast to our own. This tool is how we learn empathy, how we can recognize similarities, and behold difference with reverence. As Nin explained, "While we refuse to organize the confusions within us we will never have an objective understanding of what is happening outside… We will not be able to relate to it, to choose sides, to evaluate historically, and consequently we will be incapacitated for action."

Perhaps we should consider what it would mean not to navel-gaze. What is it to deny or ignore our navels? If we bear no mark of our maternal origin, who are we? We have been encouraged to deny our maternal genealogy in order for a single patriarchal story to grow, duplicate, and conquer, of course. If we must deny our mothers, we must also build ourselves from the clay of denying all that they represent and taught us. What would that look like? What could be situated on the polar opposite of our associations with maternity? Sadly, what much of our culture worships as powerful, as if it were a greater strength to walk through the world unencumbered by self-knowledge. To be an individual to the point of disconnect, independence in supposed objectivity, violent separation, forgetting what we learned about inter-subjective formation and existence that relies on both our differences to and cooperation with one another in favour of a cool detachment. Discouraging navel gazing is encouraging self-denial. It is an erasure. This is the stuff of sweeping ourselves under the rug in the hopes that we can begin clean. Nin explained the risk of this kind of ideology in *The Novel of the Future*:

> "[T]his persecution of the personal, of the intimate life, of the personal relationship to all things operates under two false premises: one, that it is more virtuous to give this self to the collective life; two, that it is even more virtuous to have no self at all. The taboo was on the ego, as they miscalled it, not having read the definition of ego correctly."

Nin added to this point in *On Writing*:

> "[A]lienation from the self means alienation from others. You cannot relate to others if you have no self to begin with… In order to take action full maturity in experience is required. Novels which contribute to our emotional atrophy only deepen our blindness. And nothing that we do not discover emotionally will have the power to alter our vision. The constant evasion of emotional experience has created an immaturity which turns all experience into traumatic shocks from which the human being derives no strength or development, but neurosis."

Personally, I value the wisdom delivered to us from the writers who are accused of navel-gazing, because it affords me intimacy with whole other beings and experiences unique from my own, yet connected somehow. Nin's insights are not only hers, but mine in that they nourish me, too. As Nin knew, introspection allows us to celebrate our connectedness, build bridges reaching outward, weave our own worlds into others, and understand and honor our pasts. Anaïs Nin's penetrating insights guided me in my life, so that I was also better equipped to self-reflect and journey, no longer alone as a curious girl, a developing woman, a writer—and hyper-sexed bore as well, but that's another story! How do we give birth to our own worlds and create new stories that we can, in turn, share? By staring lovingly and curiously into the fecund space between past remembrance and future potential, and conceiving of all that could be waiting there. ❖

Casandra Lim

Is that Oedipus in Anaïs Nin's *Diaries*?

Understanding Nin's work through Sigmund Freud's theory

> "And inside of this woman there was still a child without a father, a child who did not die when it should have died. There was still the ghost of a little girl forever wailing inside, bewailing the loss of a father." (Nin, *Incest* 374)

Anaïs Nin sustained an extremely complex relationship with her father, Joaquín Nin, throughout her life. The complicated nature of this relationship began unassumingly in Nin's early years with a vain childhood quest for her father's love and approval. After Joaquín's abandonment of the family when Nin was ten, her quest continued. Indeed, it advanced well into Nin's adulthood. This quest, its lack of resolution during adolescence, and its continuation into adulthood for Nin, may be explained through a simplified account of Sigmund Freud's Oedipus theory. Understanding Nin's relationship with Joaquín in this Freudian sense provides insight into the truthfulness of Nin's published non-fiction, including *Henry and June* and *Incest.*

There has been much debate over Freud's Oedipus theory, which stems in large part from his assertion that it resolves during a period of feared castration (Rand, pp. 65-66). The Oedipus theory is undeniably phallocentric, and its ability to translate the female experience has been argued inadequate (pp. 65-66). Freud's own interpretation of the resolution of the complex in females is strained; he argues that since females cannot fear castration, the Oedipus complex is difficult to resolve (p. 60).

Regardless of the underlying reason for the resolution of the complex, phallocentric or not, it may be argued that many children generally do enter into a phase of development when they seek affection from the opposite-sex parent in the Freudian sense, and for this reason, the term Oedipus complex will be used herein.

Oedipus and Joaquín Nin

In popular culture, Sigmund Freud's Oedipus theory is generally used negatively to describe individuals with ardent connections to a parent of the opposite gender. However, Freud argues that the theory applies to each individual during the natural course of development (Mitchell & Black, p. 15). Freud first claims that at approximately five or six years of age, a child will identify the parent of the opposite sex as a love-object (p. 15). "Like Sophocles's Oedipus, each child is destined to follow her desires and thereby become caught in a powerful, passionate drama with no easy resolution" (p. 15). Thus, during these early years, Freud argues that all children become fascinated with the parent of the opposite gender in both an affectionate and a sexual way.

Nin's early relationship with Joaquín, though strained, paralleled the initial pattern of Freud's developmental theory of sexuality. Nin writes in *Henry and June*, "My father did not want a girl. He said I was ugly. When I wrote or drew something, he did not believe it was my work. I never remember a caress or a compliment from him, except when I nearly died at the age of nine" (p. 115). In this passage, written years later, Nin's natural childhood desire for her father's approval is clear. Nin recalls her unrequited love for him, painfully recording that she "never remember[s] a caress or compliment from him," and that he called her "ugly." Joaquín's harsh criticism only furthered Nin's Oedipal longing for his love and approval.

Freud goes on to argue that in children who follow a normal path of development, the resolution of the Oedipus complex is derived from, in very general terms, separation from one's parents (Freud, Part III, Lecture XXI). This separation involves the child overcoming sexual desire for the parent in order to seek an external love object (Part III, Lecture XXI). According to Freud, a child's adolescence will ordinarily begin detachment from the father or mother who has previously held the role of love-object (Part III, Lecture XXI). Freud may have been incorrect about the universal cause for this separation, a fear of castration, but it does seem that a separation from one's parents generally takes place to some degree during adolescence. During this separation, the child's desire for solely parental approval and love declines.

While Nin's childhood desire for her father's affection followed the normal progression of Freud's theory, Joaquín's abandonment of the family affected the potential resolution of Nin's misplaced desire. When Nin was ten, Joaquín Nin left his family for another woman (Henke, p. 120). Though Nin was on the cusp of adolescence, after Joaquín's departure, her devotion continued. This persistent desire for Joaquín's love and approval is evident in Nin's response to Joaquín's correspondence to her grandparents. In one such letter, Joaquín told his parents that he hoped his children would always value their French heritage, and that it was only proper that they speak French in the home (Bair, p. 25). Even after the family arrived in America, Nin took these suggestions very literally and refused to speak or write any language other than French (pp. 26-27). Her French never developed past that of an elementary nature because she had no way of expanding upon her vocabulary or grammar in the United States, and she "struggle[d] to write in a French that remained babyish as she matured into an American adolescent" (p. 34). Even though her father was not present to witness such devotion, the burgeoning adolescent retained her belief that if she acted only to please him, he may have bestowed affection upon her.

Around a year later, eleven-year-old Nin began writing letters to Joaquín (Bair, p. 25). Most of the letters were then copied into a journal, which evolved into her celebrated *Diary* (p. 25). The fact that Nin first began the diary as a collection of letters to her father poses many interesting questions. Nin later revealed in an interview with Keith Berwick that

> Originally, though, [the diary] was intended for my father. That puts a slightly different slant on it. I began it at eleven, and I meant it to be a journal of the journey to America, a strange country that he feared… I was going to make such a description of it as to entice him to come back to the family." (DuBow, p. 59)

Here, she herself admits that this fact "puts a slightly different slant on [the diary]." Hence, the first diaries were letters to Joaquín in which Nin attempted to persuade him to return to the family. Appreciating these circumstances surrounding the beginning of Nin's work is valuable in understanding her non-fiction.

Even if Nin's audience changed from the external to the internal, she still may have subconsciously been writing for "the absent and idealized parent of childhood fantasy" (Henke, p. 121) since that was for whom the diary was originally intended. The writing traditions and choice of material established in the first journal may have carried over to later volumes. This prior consciousness of writing for her father may have altered not only how she described people, particularly herself, and events within the diary, but also which material she chose to include in the diary. As explained by Jean Owen, "In some ways, we lose sight of this original *love-letter* as the diary—meant to bring someone back—gradually comes to stand in for the absent father" (Owen). In this way, it appears as though Nin was not only trying originally to validate America in order to prompt Joaquín's return to the family, but was also attempting to alter his perception of her.

Unresolved desires and choice of written material

In the unexpurgated diaries *Henry and June* and *Incest*, it becomes clear that Nin's father not only permeates many of her thoughts as a child, but also well into her married life. This continued fixation affected the contents of the diaries: the events, the interpretation of others' and her own feelings. In making these choices, Nin was continuously looking to convince herself—and subconsciously her father—of her self-worth and desirability. She admitted later, though without acknowledging a lingering Oedipus complex, "I had to build my confidence which was thoroughly destroyed by my father. He left me nothing at all" (DuBow, p. 75).

Nin's inclusion of seemingly insignificant events may be understood through her desire for her father's approval, including many passages detailing external compliments. For example, in the following passage from *Incest*, Nin describes herself as a beautiful woman to be admired:

> Emilia goes to clean the bathroom after I have taken a bath and says, "It is so wonderful to go into the bathroom after the *señora* has been there; it smells good—fragrant—and before, the other two ladies I worked for—after their baths, I hated to go in, it was so smelly."
>
> Emilia's adoration of me is based on my "goodness," on my "strangeness," and on my "beauty." She loves to touch my hand because it is silky, she admires my elegance, my ideas, my tallness. She collects all the photos of me which I throw away, and has them in her bedroom. (*Incest*, p.77)

These two seemingly inconsequential details—her maid's comments to her after she bathes and the fact that her maid retains her discarded personal photographs convey her need to feel desired and to be recognized for her "beauty and "elegance."

Similarly, Nin quotes June Miller saying to her, "I thought your eyes were blue. They are strange and beautiful, gray and gold, with those long black lashes. You are the most graceful woman I have ever seen" (*Henry and June*, p. 17). Here, Nin is presumably writing for herself, without the thought of publication in mind. Yet, she establishes herself as a desirable person with admirable physical traits. Nin not only acknowledges another's compliment, but implies that she is most deserving of the praise.

The inclusion of these passages in the diary suggests that Nin is reaffirming to herself that she is indeed desirable. This need to be desired or admired is mirrored in Nin's longing for her father's approval and love during childhood, and it persists well into adulthood.

Nin's diary also gives special attention to compliments (both internal and external) regarding aspects of her character, predominately those relating to her work and creativity. For instance, in *Henry and June*, she compares her work with Henry Miller's, stating,

> I see now that some of the pages I have written on June, simply and humanly penetrating, are greater as art than Henry's deformations... About both June and Henry, I have been more human, more comprehending, more true, and perhaps, I may in the end be more artistic. (p. 30)

Nin not only recognizes the depth of her literary descriptions of the Millers, but praises herself for it. She concludes by suggesting she may be more artistic than Miller, attempting to affirm her artistic worth.

But Nin also includes her feelings of inadequacies. She describes in *Incest*:

> I have been ill—ill with morbidities, obsessions, susceptibilities, I am perpetually hurt by something or other—trifles—I cannot free myself.

> I feel that people mock me, overlook me, misunderstand me. I add up small grievances and forget all the admirations, compliments, triumphs. Anger at a small offense blots out all the day. If Andre [de Vilmorin] is ironic, I fear it is at my expense. I feel I don't talk well, that my irony only appears in my writing. If Louise forgets to offer me a cigarette, I am hurt. Lillian's hostility distresses me. I am jealous of Henry's writing so much about Lowenfels when I can predict that someday [Walter] Lowenfels will crumble. (p. 266)

It is apparent that Nin feels a lack of approval and greatly desires it. Her focus on "trifles" and not on accomplishments illustrates how she filters out all non-critical responses. She rationalizes that she has great "admirations, compliments, [and] triumphs," yet she cannot appreciate these successes. Are these feelings spawned by the fact her father's approval has not yet been attained?

Truthfulness with an Oedipal lens

It is evident that Nin developed and maintained for a period of time an ideal notion of her father, which can be explained through her unresolved Oedipus complex, as depicted in *Henry and June* and *Incest*. When Joaquín abandoned his family during Nin's early adolescence, Nin believed him to be an almost divine figure and longed for his affection. With his departure, she was denied the opportunity to identify him as a human being with human weaknesses, and for this reason, her desire for her father's love continued well beyond her adolescence.

An understanding of Nin's relationship with her father is central to accurately interpreting her work and to recognizing its authenticity. The narrative of the diaries, first begun for Joaquín, is truthful; yet, the choice of recorded incidents and impressions is dependent upon Nin's desired effect in writing—originally to gain her father's approval and affection. Reading *Henry and June* and *Incest* with this awareness allows for further appreciation of the diaries' meaning and their truthfulness.

While Nin spent much of her life longing for her father and his approval from a distance, she did reunite with him in 1933 (Bair, pp. 161, 170). During this time, as described in *Incest*, they engaged in an incestuous affair (*Incest*, p. 209). This literal climax of her Oedipal desires brought about changes in Nin, one of which was the realization of her father's humanness. She writes in *Incest*, "But my Father is nonhuman and should have been God. He is the one who has imposed perfection, who has initiated the gods, who has no love of human naturalness. But in the end he is like me, a hypocrite" (p. 283). She acknowledges that Joaquín attempts to portray himself as perfect, but, in reality, bears human flaws. This realization provides Nin with knowledge necessary to begin to resolve her Oedipal desire for her father, and later, her rejection of him. ❖

Works cited

Bair, Deidre. *Anaïs Nin: A Biography*. New York: Putnam, 1995.

DuBow, Wendy, Ed. *Conversations with Anaïs Nin*. Jackson, MS: University Press of Mississippi, 1994.

Freud, Sigmund. *A General Introduction to Psychoanalysis*. CreateSpace Independent Publishing Platform, 2016. Kindle edition.

Henke, Suzette. "Anaïs Nin's *Journal of Love*: Father-Loss and Incestuous Desire." *Anaïs Nin, Literary Perspectives*, ed. Suzanne Nalbantian. New York: Palgrave Macmillan, 1997, pp. 120-135.

Mitchell, Stephen A. and Margaret J. Black. *Freud and Beyond: A History of Modern Psychoanalytic Thought*. New York: Basic Books, 1995.

Nin, Anaïs. *Henry and June*. 1986. San Diego; London; New York: A Harvest Book, Harcourt, 1989.

----. *Incest*. San Diego; London; New York: A Harvest Book, Harcourt, 1992.

Owen, Jean. "Uncanny Echoes: Anaïs Nin's narrative of incest." A *Café in Space: The Anaïs Nin Literary Journal* vol. 11. San Antonio, TX: Sky Blue Press, 2014. Kindle edition.

Rand, Nicholas. "Did Women Threaten the Oedipus Complex Between 1922 and 1933?: Freud's Battle with Universality and its Aftermath in the Work of K. Horney and M. Torok." *Angelaki: journal of the theoretical humanities* vol. 9, no. 1. London, Routledge: 2004, pp. 53-66.

David Green

Out in the Midi Sun

Adventures in Lawrence Durrell country

> *Journeys, like artists, are born and not made. A thousand differing circumstances contribute to them, few of them determined by the will—whatever we may think. They flower spontaneously out of the demands of our natures—and the best of them lead us not only outwards in space, but inwards as well. Travel can be one the most rewarding forms of introspection.*
>
> —*Bitter Lemons* (1957)

The impulse to travel is particularly strong in Australians. We live, to quote former prime minister, Paul Keating, "at the arse end of the world," but many of us have recent origins in other places—or literary and historical interests that see us longing for the European experience: the landscape, people, and atmospheres of our cultural heritage. But tourism needs a spine. Effective travel requires backbone, motive. Lawrence Durrell provided one. He is a writer with whom I have felt an almost personal connection, and about whom, along with Henry Miller, I have made a program for ABC Radio, *Lawrence Durrell and Henry Miller: A Wartime Correspondence.*

Specifically, I wanted to explore the "spirit of place" surrounding the two houses in Provence, in which Durrell spent the last third of his life and where he wrote his major works. I was keen to experience in a direct physical sense, rather than as an abstract concept, the effect these places may have had on his writing.

I had been to Durrell sites in Corfu, the Greek Islands, London, Paris, Crete, even Bournemouth, but Provence remained largely unexplored; a place of history, myth and legend. The ancient land of Oc, a realm of olives and vines and the place where Lawrence Durrell lived for thirtythree years and wrote his most famous works in a flood of creativity, which, even if begun elsewhere, came to fruition in this stony, cicada-singing landscape, helping him to become the artist he longed to be. With the aid of maps, brochures, online bookings and advice from our French friends Catherine and Bienvenido, who lived near Nîmes and knew Lawrence Durrell-country well, Denise and I roughed out our itinerary and set off for France in June, 2015.

After a few days in Paris exploring places old and new, our friends, Catherine and Bienvenido arrived from Avignon. With them we began two days of intense tourism under warming skies. As a priority we set out to discover Henry Miller, Anaïs Nin and Lawrence Durrell's terrace in the Villa Seurat near Alesia. However, we forgot to bring the actual address so the house remained a mystery. We asked a local man heading out for the day, if he knew which house Miller and Durrell had lived in. He looked puzzled then said, "Ah, that, I think, was a long time ago."

Number 18 Villa Seurat is an unremarkable off-white Art Deco terrace towards the end of the street on the left. Here, in 1937 budding writer Durrell and his first wife Nancy teamed up with *Tropic of Cancer* author Henry Miller and Anaïs Nin who was to become famous for her diaries. The "Three Musketeers," as Durrell, Miller and Nin styled themselves, spent their evenings drinking and talking long into the night and their days exploring Paris, writing and running *Booster*, a low key literary magazine. There is a photo of Miller in a great coat striking some contemplative pose outside a neighbouring house near the cul de sac. In homage I struck a similar pose. After too many photos we continued on past the Luxembourg, down through the Latin Quarter, the Sorbonne, then across the Seine past Notre Dame, and on to the Arc de Triomphe.

An outdoor lunch turned into a humorous affair. While we ate, an elderly woman of frail and unkempt appearance loomed close and began ranting. She moved strategically from point to point, continuing her salvos of invective. The waiters shrugged in a Gallic way, the French diners muttered over their *pommes frites*. Then she disappeared. "What was that about?" I asked Catherine. "Oh, she said many things, but mainly that she had lived in this area for fifty years (she looked seventy-five) and was a true Parisienne, while we were just tourists and imposters." Maybe it was time to head south.

> *The southbound train from Paris was the one we had taken from time immemorial—the same long slowcoach of a train, stringing out its bluish lights across the twilight landscape like some super glow worm. It reached Provence at dawn, often by brindled moonlight which striped the countryside like a tiger's hide.*
>
> —*Monsieur* (1974)

So Durrell's *Avignon Quintet* begins with a train journey from Paris to Avignon. By contrast, we began our journey south on France's famous TVG, which covers the 700 odd kilometres from Paris to Nîmes in three hours. Even in these comfortable carriages you feel the speed. In fact, for a brief period I felt vague motion sickness, which passed after a restorative can of cold Dutch lager. The countryside certainly does whirr by, and you pass cars on motorways with ease.

> *Somewhere between Calabria and Corfu the blue really begins. All the way across Italy you find yourself moving through a landscape severely domesticated—each valley laid out after the architect's pattern, brilliantly lighted, human. But once you strike out from the flat, desolate Calabrian mainland towards the sea, you are aware of a change in the heart of things:*

aware of the horizon beginning to stain at the rim of the world: aware of islands coming out of the darkness to meet you.

—*Prospero's Cell* (1945)

And somewhere south of Lyon you begin to feel a change in landscape and sky. Vines appear. The broad, rolling wheat fields, scattered farmsteads, and pale skies of the north give way to low, rugged hills, sprawling red-tiled villages, orchards and thicker blue above sun-baked fields. You become conscious of a landscape with olive trees moving northward to meet you.

Later that day Catherine and Bienvenido, who were to be our drivers, guides and translators, drove us to the Mazet Dodo just outside Nîmes. As we turned off the Nîmes-to-Uzès road and entered a narrow semi-rural valley cut by dry stone walls, shaded by olive trees and tall pines, studded with yellow broom and set with rustic houses in unkempt yards, I sensed we were approaching a certain destiny. Our excitement was palpable. Alan Thomas, Durrell's friend and bibliographer describes the scene as it was when Durrell moved there:

The Mazet Michel is situated in an area which was rich in olive trees until, some years ago, they were all killed by a ferocious frost. The district immediately around looks rather stark, littered with millions of slabs of stone, gleaming in the sun, and dotted with thousands of apparently dead trunks.

—*Spirit of Place,* p. 132

Although the higher slopes of the little valley are stony and some dead trunks remain, most of the area carries healthy foliage and the olives are much recovered. We had both expected the area to be more isolated than it was. The rustic seclusion which had brought Durrell here had been replaced by a degree of semi-urbanization that the Dodo's online brochure had failed to mention; there was the dance studio in the barn next door with mums and teenage daughters coming and going all afternoon. We also discovered that the French army has a firing range on the nearby *garrigue*. Bursts of automatic weapons fire were not uncommon; so much for rustic isolation on the outskirts of Nîmes.

But, we were in Lawrence Durrell country, his old *mazet* just across the road behind high stone walls and large iron gates. And the Mazet Dodo had been on his land. Under blue skies and a warm sun our mood improved as we settled in. The dry heat and then the soft evenings reminded me of Canberra in summer: the smell of the dry grass and dust as the evening sky grows dim, the cool air sharpening the senses, becoming conscious of dogs barking far off, feeling the stillness falling to a breathless hush as the colors thicken and dim in a slow dusk and birds falling silent one by one.

We dine late by candlelight, the light almost as yellow as the moon outside the great windows of the dining room, portraits of Venetian ancestors stare pallidly at us from the walls in their mouldering frames.

—*Prospero's Cell* (1945)

David Green at the Durrell Wall

We also dine late under candlelight, the flames unwavering on an evening reminiscent of those described by Durrell on Corfu, where in the silence behind Count D, you can hear the soft plop of orchard fruit upon the ground. The fare this evening is oysters, salad, bread (of course) and rosé wine set on a plain wooden table. With our friends, Catherine and Bienvenido, we discuss travel, the parlous state of France, Lawrence Durrell, and plans for the next day. Earlier that day, Beatrice, whose Air B & B barn we were renting, told us that Lawrence bought the Mazet Michel because the house and the valley reminded him of Greece. Later, he gifted the place to his brother, Gerald. After Gerald died in 1994, his wife Lee owned the place. A few years later, a British diplomat bought Mazet Michel at about the same time that Beatrice bought the cottage and barn. I had noticed that the *mazet* is now called the *Mas* Michel. I asked Catherine to explain the difference between *mas* and *mazet*. "Oh, it is very simple. One is bigger than the other."

Mas Michel loomed across the road, so close but so far. We could see the garden, the stone walls, the pool fence and parts of the house, but, as Alan

Thomas observed "the *mazet* lay within a fortified *enceinte*" (p. 132)—high stone walls, thick brambles, and a tall black iron gate. It was here, in semi-rural isolation, that Durrell had his happiest and most productive years. According to his biographers, Ian MacNiven and Gordon Bowker, his third wife, Claude Vincendon, whom he met on Cyprus, was the love of his life. She understood him and could handle his "creative madness" in a way his other wives could not. With her inspiration and editorial assistance, Durrell completed at the *mazet* the four-volume novel sequence *The Alexandria Quartet*, which shot him to fame in literary and artistic circles in the mid-1960s. The significance of the *mazet* to this process is not to be underestimated. Before leaving Cyprus in 1956 Durrell told Penelope Tremayne, a poet friend:

> *"When I leave here I am going to live in the south of France, where the cigarettes are a shilling a packet and wine is sixpence a bottle, and I have got enough in the kitty to live for a year like that by the end of which I shall have a written a book that will really sell...so I am going to write high-brow pornography and they'll swallow it."*
>
> —Bowker, p. 231

After a few rental properties in Sommières, Claude and Lawrence found the rustic Mazet Michel near Nîmes in 1958 and bought the place in 1959. Due to the nearby firing range it was cheap. It also came with a large parcel of land which offered seclusion from the outside world, the perfect place for an emerging author and his new wife.

Mas Michel

Unable at this stage to make further explorations of Mas Michel, we spent a few days exploring the region—the Camargue cowboy country, the seaside town of Saintes-Maries-de-la-Mer, where Durrell liked to go swimming and Avignon, the setting for the *Quintet*. One afternoon, pulling up at our Mazet Dodo late in the afternoon, we heard English voices from the driveway of the Mas Michel. Catherine said, "Quick David, go talk to them!"

Well, I had been sipping Chateau San Pellegrino rosé (wine in a mineral water bottle) on the dusty drive over from Avignon—so, thus emboldened, I ran over the Chemin des Calvas and up the driveway where a group of posh-sounding Englishmen were maneuvering a large trailer from which an old Austin Healey had just been unloaded. The classic car was in mint condition. The owners, I later learned, were heading off on a rally through Italy. "Hello, Monsieur! Je suis un aficionado de Lawrence Durrell," I called up the driveway to a summer-clad man of about 60 who, properly English, was possibly the diplomat we had been told about. "I'm David Green from Australia. I'm doing a Lawrence Durrell tour of Provence. I believe he used to live here?"

The man turned away from the parking operation, focused his gaze on this antipodean invasion and said, after a pause, "Do you know you are the first Durrell person ever to have come here?" This astonished me, as did his next sentence: "Right! Well, I suppose you had better come in and have a drink."

I'd expected an Oxford-intoned "bugger off!" So, what could I say but "sure." The Austin Healey purred into life and rolled down the driveway, and as the English friends departed, we—Denise, followed by Catherine and then Bienvenido—began an assault on the *mas*. We were all cordially invited to drinks on the terrace by Noel and his old school-friend, Bryce Sutcliffe, an Irish-born American. The fortress had been breached, achieved by a combination of boldness, hospitality and alcohol. What a mix. For me, to stand on that terrace, see that house and that view, was intoxicating and not easy to describe, but *The Paris Review* got it pretty right:

> *It is a peasant cottage with four rooms to which he has added a bathroom and a lavatory. The sitting-room, where the interview was held, has a large fireplace and a French window leading onto a terrace constructed by Durrell himself. From the terrace one has a view of the small valley at the end of which he lives.*
>
> —"The Art of Fiction XXIII," p. 33

The wine and talk flowed spontaneously, tours of the house and garden followed including the old shepherd's hut where Larry used to burn rubbish and "the Garden Louisa," named after Larry's mother. The original *mazet* bought by Larry and Claude in 1959 remains intact but has been extended, first by Larry and later by his brother, who created a new wing, so to speak. Noel has made some alterations of his own to accommodate his family and to bring in some modern amenities, including a fifteen-meter pool. He has owned the place for about seventeen years after purchasing it, in three stages, from Lee Durrell (Gerald's widow). In 1997 Noel first bought the *mazet* and 8,000 square feet, then added the 1,000 square foot "Forest Louisa." Finally, in March 1998, Noel acquired the rest of the land on the east side of the Chemin des Calvas. The Durrell land on the west side has gone to others, including Beatrice of the Mazet Dodo. With the acquisition came most of the original furnishings. The big fireplace still works. Gerry's favorite chair is there and so is the old cistern in which they used to "swim." Noel conducted a complete tour of the property, and as we walked, he spoke of future plans that came from a man with seemingly deep pockets and one who clearly loved the place and had a great respect for the former owners. Of the purchase, he said, "Lee was marvellous. An American but an English rose nonetheless."

Back on the terrace a crisis had emerged. Noel said, "I've only got one more bottle of wine!" Agape, we all looked at each other. Bienvenido came to the rescue with another bottle of Chateau Pellegrino. Before long, this too had gone. As tongues loosened and bonhomie increased, to my great delight, Noel invited us to dinner on the terrace.

"The problem is, it was just going to be Bryce and me. There isn't much, just some cannelloni and strawberries and cream."

"A case of loaves and fishes?" I replied.

Noel looked around for help. Then Denise and Catherine offered to drive into Nîmes to the *marché* of Mustafa, known to Catherine as "Mustafa cash only," for reinforcements.

The evening evolved into a fiesta. Dinner, hastily prepared by Bryce and Bienvenido, consisted of salad, vongole and pasta, olives, cannelloni, eggs with mayonnaise, salami and melon draped with Parma, and, of course, baguettes, followed by the promised strawberries and cream—all served on the terrace under lamplight on what was once Lawrence's old timber table and washed down with fresh bottles of rosé. In between talk of the Durrells and other obscure subjects, Noel kept apologising for his lack of hospitality. Hardly his fault that on a quiet summer's evening his peace had been shattered by three garrulous Australians and a guitar-wielding Spaniard. Bryce ribbed him gently as old friends do (and spoke knowledgeably about world affairs). Catherine and Bienvenido enlivened the air with local gossip and humorous stories. There was laughter, discussions, toasts to the Durrells, for Noel is himself a fan of the brothers Durrell and has a fine collection of their books left to him when he bought the place. He is also conscientious about maintaining the property in the spirit of the Durrell family.

Then Bienvenido's guitar came out. Flamenco and songs *des paysans* began, dancing too, and the wine continued to flow. Noel said he was delighted to meet such enthusiasts and offered us the use of the swimming pool for the rest of our stay (he being off to England in the morning). The night ended in great merriment, oaths of friendship and exchange of details. As Noel said, we dined in a manner of which Larry would have heartily approved. Renata Vassiliou, who worked for Larry in the 1970s, said to me in a letter of 2009:

> *He used to start the white wine at 10 o'clock and then sat down to give a mini concert while I was fighting with his typewriter. His brother Gerry very much liked the Gigondas Cote du Rhone (15%) and so did I. I remember the "joyeuse ambience" at the birthday of Lee Durrell in the Nîmes Mazet one year when Gerry and Lee stayed for several months.*

A "joyeuse ambience" indeed—a night never to be forgotten by those who remember it. I went to bed that night hoping that the spirits of Larry and Gerry were smiling down on us from somewhere amongst the stars.

Vampire House

> *This house was bought by Claude (in 1966) at a Paris auction. She died shortly after they moved in, and while Durrell continued to live there, he later complained that it was haunted by too many ghosts.*
>
> —Bowker, *The Dark Labyrinth*, illus. Route 15 de Saussines

Two days after the party at *Mas* Michel, we drove over to Sommières to find the "Vampire House." Having seen the appeal of the little valley below the *garrigue*—which I felt to be very much keeping with Larry's character and his ideas of the right Mediterranean landscape—why his move to Sommières and that big, gloomy house? Aristocratic pretensions, an arrival statement, more rooms for guests? To judge from the black and white photos, it looked more like a setting for an Edgar Allan Poe story than for a man who loved wine and sun. As we drove I asked Catherine about Sommières.

"Sommières," she said, "is one of the poorest villages in France, but it's nice in a dilapidated way. Anyway there's an old Roman bridge and lots of narrow streets, very medieval."

What had drawn Durrell here? Cheap real estate? The Vidourle River, the greener countryside, or the fact that, despite being a medieval trading town with a Roman bridge, Sommières is off the tourist trail—a working town not tricked up, like Uzès, for visitors with deep pockets? Maybe Claude (and Larry) were sick of roughing it at the *mazet* and needed a bigger party house? Claude had aristocratic origins in Alexandria. After all, it was she who bought the house.

A medieval town asleep on its feet.

So Durrell wrote to Miller in a letter in 1957. This proved an apt description as did Catherine's comments about poverty. The narrow streets huddling around little squares are charming, until you realise that the streets need repair, the walls are peeling, the shutters stained and old, and the houses small. From the tourist office we got a small map and brochure that mentioned the famous author, though not in the most accurate detail, and set off across the Vidourle, where, in a scene that would have pleased Larry, local children were diving into the slow, green waters. But as we made our way across the bridge, I thought, "You know, in the world of literary tourism, where is Lawrence Durrell? He's certainly not up there with Wordsworth or Jane Austen."

In stark contrast to the Mas Michel, number 15 rue de Saussines stands at the confluence of two busy roads about a stone's throw from the town centre. Durrell's house turned out to be larger than expected—a three-storey "gentleman's home," as might befit a writer of means. Alan Thomas describes the house as "a quite large nineteenth-century house, somewhat mysterious and romantic, hidden behind high walls" (*Spirit of Place*, p. 134).

The grounds and interior weren't easy to assess. I had to climb walls and peer through bushes. I am sure the aristocratic Claude, and later Ghislaine de Boysson, would have been at home here. Stylish, imposing, and gothic, the mansion has a large, green, well-treed garden and outer defenses that would take cannon to breach. It has strong security measures. A code panel and four letterboxes suggest separate apartments. And although Durrell mentions a swimming pool in his writings, I saw no evidence of one now. Although I could imagine Larry entertaining there in style or having weekend house parties, the "Vampire House" is a far cry from the Larry of Greece: the white house at Kalami on Corfu, the Villa Cleobulus on Rhodes, the old peasant house in Bellapais, Cyprus. The Mas Michel captured and recalled these places. Even today, the *mas* is far more secluded and, to me, represents the Durrell of the island books and happy memories. The Vampire House was at odds with the sparkling Mediterranean world evoked so magically in the island books and in poems like "This Unimportant Morning":

This unimportant morning
Something goes singing where
The capes turn over on their sides
And the warm Adriatic rides
Her blue and sun washing
At the edge of the world and its brilliant cliffs.
Day rings in the higher airs
Pure with cicadas, and slowing
Like a pulse to smoke from farms,
Extinguished in the exhausted earth,
Unclenched like a fist and going.

—*Collected Poems*

No. 15 Route de Saussines is the gloomy pile in which Durrell lived from 1967 until his death in 1990, age 78. Claude died prematurely of cancer at 7:10 on January 1, 1967. Apparently, Durrell stopped the hands of the wall clock and did not reset them (MacNiven, p. 553). Durrell considered selling the house which he later described in *Sicilian Carousel* as "my old bat-haunted house in Provence." There is no doubt Claude's death altered his mindscape for the worse. Claudine Brelet, a writer and photographer who visited in May 1968, claimed, "Larry's spirits needed a lift…the blinds were all locked and an immense sadness impregnated the whole house." She then went around "*la maison Dracula*" as he had come to call the place, opening all the shutters (MacNiven, p. 566).

Here he wrote *Tunc* and *Nunqham*, novels which mark a shift in Durrell's writing towards darker, more introverted themes, spiced up with ribald humour. *The Avignon Quintet* (1971-1985), Durrell's last major series of books, developed this trend further. These are a mysterious series of novels set in World War II exploring themes of fiction versus reality, human identity, sexuality and suicide against a backdrop of Gnostic sects and the heresy of the Knights Templar. Patrick Parrinder in the *London Review of Books*, described *The Avignon Quintet* as "an enigmatic and secretive work, a cluster of dark passages and gaudy treasure filled caves" (p. 22). My own sentence for it, based on our visit to Avignon is "darkness in the sunlight." Underneath that bright, Biscuit-colored landscape, there a long, often violent past.

The "Vampire House"

There is consensus with which I agree, that at Mas Michel, Durrell had his happiest years and completed his best works, *Bitter Lemons* and the *Quartet*. The house at Sommières is a grander but sadder place, reflective of the man himself when he lived there. Durrell achieved fame in his lifetime, even relished it. But it came at a price, one he recognized. Towards the end of his life, Larry set a poem, "Route Saussine 15," in *Caesar's Vast Ghost*. Its opening lines sadden the reader:

Only of late have I come to see this house
As something poisoned when I paid for it;
Its beauty was specious and it hid pure grief.
Your absence, dearest, brings it no relief.

Had Larry lived out his days at the Mazet Michel, I wonder if he could have ever written such lines? I doubt it. If Durrell is famous for writing about *spirit of place*, he was, of course, greatly influenced by it. Visiting these two very different houses in Provence made me very aware of that: one simple, sunny, spare and Mediterranean, the other grand, gothic, northern. It may well be that the dark corridors of the Vampire House, with its bats and often empty rooms, seeped into Durrell's mind over time and colored with grimmer hues his later work. I know which house I preferred.

The morning of our departure for Paris, I went swimming in the pool at the *mas*. As I lapped, I reflected on Larry's love of swimming and my own, on Larry's love of wine and my own. Breast-stroking past those rooms in which Gerry had caroused; looking up at the stone terraces and paths where Larry had entertained; where Paddy Fermor, Diana Gould, Alan Thomas and others had walked and talked and drank and laughed was truly moving. Then a strange chemical reaction seemed to take place within.

I could see Larry leaning on the stone wall above, the one he had himself built, smoking a cigarette, watching me with a quiet, knowing air. "You should have stayed here, Larry," I thought—and then he was gone. ❖

Works cited

Bowker, Gordon. *Through the Dark Labyrinth: A Biography of Lawrence Durrell.* London: Pimlico, 1998.

Durrell, Lawrence. "The Art of Fiction XXIII: Lawrence Durrell." Interviewed by Gene Andrewski and Julian Mitchell. *The Paris Review* 22 (Autumn-Winter 1960): pp. 32-61.

----. *The Avignon Quintet: Monsieur, Livia, Constance, Sebastian, Quinx.* London: Faber, 1992.

----. *Bitter Lemons.* London: Faber, 1957.

----. *Caesar's Vast Ghost*: Aspects of Provence. New York: Arcade, 1990.

----. *Prospero's Cell: A Guide to the Landscape and Manners of the Island of Corcyra.* London: Faber, 1945.

----. *Sicilian Carousel*: Axiom Press, Virginia, 1977.

----. *Spirit of Place: Letters and Essays on Travel.* Ed. Alan G. Thomas. New York: Dutton, 1969.

Durrell, Lawrence, and Henry Miller. *The Durrell-Miller Letters, 1935-80.* Ed. Ian S. MacNiven. New York: New Directions, 1988.

MacNiven, Ian. *Lawrence Durrell: A biography.* London: Faber, 1998.

Parrinder, Patrick. Rev. of *The Avignon Quintet*, by Lawrence Durrell. *London Review of Books*, 6 June 1985: pp. 22-23.

Vassiliou, Renata. Letter to the author, 2009.

Tristine Rainer

Remembering John Ferrone

Anaïs Nin introduced me to John Ferrone, her Harcourt Brace Jovanovich editor, at her Silverlake, California house where she lived as the wife of Rupert Pole. John, a New Yorker, knew her other husband, Hugo Guiler, as well, and was privy to the secret of Anaïs's double life. As one of the most graceful men I have known, both in his manner and his movements, he was at ease in the world of sexual/emotional discretion. He'd lived the life of an undisguised gay man of 1950s New York, and it was a world he negotiated with integrity and subtlety.

In 1978, when I published my first book, *The New Diary*, in hardbound, John made an offer to my publisher, Jeremy Tarcher, for Harcourt to acquire the paperback rights. Although he was contractually obligated to inform me of the offer, Tarcher, without my knowledge, rejected it out of hand. When later I learned from John that he'd made the trade paperback offer while no one had told me, he was outraged. He was a genteel literary editor, a breed that has all but disappeared, a man of honor who pledged his impressive gifts to enhance the work of his authors and stay in the background. He was modest about the vast improvements he made in Anaïs Nin's prose.

Anaïs, who most valued spontaneity in writing, once told me, dismissively flicking her fingers, "Punctuation, grammar, that's for editors." John did far more than correct her unschooled grammar and punctuation, though. He highlighted the intelligence and emotional wisdom in her outpourings while giving her work an aesthetic subtlety it would otherwise lack.

Because of his commitment to make Anaïs's writing shine in the best light, John's relationship with Rupert became antagonistic after her death. Each man complained to me about the other. Rupert wanted to preserve Anaïs's every word as she wrote it. He was working with John on Harcourt's publication of her posthumous erotic work. John was dedicated to making her writing as honed as possible, which required cutting and shaping. They both loved her and her memory and, as with so many people who have loved her or her work, felt an almost irrational exclusive ownership of her.

Yet on another occasion I recall an evening when John and Rupert were as jovial as two teenage buddies together. I was then in my thirties and working as President of Grand Central Films, a co-venture between Thames Television and an American production company. I wanted to option the *Diaries* as a network television mini-series. Since John was visiting L.A. and I then had an unlimited expense account, I invited John and Rupert to an expensive trendy restaurant near Paramount. They were adorable, each vying to be the most charming and witty, like competing beaus. Anaïs was gone, but her flirtatious spirit was with us that night.

In later years I would phone John when I visited New York and he would always make time to take me to lunch or dinner or, even better, cook for me. We both enjoyed literary gossip and swapping stories about Anaïs's foibles and secrets. He was lonely after his partner died, and for such a reserved gentleman, warm and vulnerable when he talked about the importance—the centrality—of love in our lives.

I recall only one disagreement between John and myself; it was just a half-full/half empty difference in perspective. I had been admiring Anaïs's tenacity in working on herself, in transforming herself from a neurotic, frustrated unpublished writer into a joyous woman who shared her hard-won success and wisdom with others. John bemoaned that Anaïs enjoyed the publication of her *Diaries* and her emotional equanimity so late in her life. "She only had a few years before knowledge of her cancer ruined it," he said. "It took her so long to get what she wanted. She enjoyed it so briefly."

"But she got there. She realized her dreams," I said.

He shook his head. "Too briefly."

I understand those feelings now, John. You had a relatively long life, living despite Parkinson's Disease to 91. My regret is that our friendship blossomed only in your later years and lasted too briefly, too briefly. ❖

John Ferrone and Anaïs Nin, 1970s

Lana Fox

L'Étalon

Erotica inspired by Anaïs Nin's Auletris

Adrienne had never seen her neighbor smile. All she felt when they passed one another was serious intensity. He had a wide mouth, this neighbor, with lips so long that his smile would surely be legendary, revealing more of those white teeth than he'd ever shown. If he smiled, he'd seem warmer, more human perhaps. If he smiled, he would not seem so raw. He was animal, *la bête*, like sex itself.

The kind of man she'd been taught to avoid.

He lived in the apartment opposite hers and his door had a habit of falling open. It didn't seem to possess a lock, which shocked Adrienne. She wondered if he was often robbed, for his place was plain and he seemed to have little furniture. Late at night, when she'd get home from work, she'd often arrive to hear a soft, pleasurable moaning coming from his apartment. A timid virgin, she was ashamed that she enjoyed the sound and was fearful of the dreadful power such likings might unlock in her, but still she'd sneak up to his front door and gaze into his one-room apartment, where his double bed dominated the scene. Sometimes, she'd see him kissing a woman, tangling his fingers in her hair, biting her lips every now and then, and because this sight aroused Adrienne, it also usually frightened her away.

One night, however, things changed. She arrived to find her neighbor was already having sex, and, in spite of her shame, she found herself fascinated. Her neighbor was holding a pale-skinned, naked woman from behind, taking her savagely, his hands grasping her bare hips as he thrust his sex into hers. This woman was crying out ecstatically with his every lunge, her face turned up towards the ceiling, her jaw slack as she quivered with pleasure. "You are large!" she cried out. The largest!" Her pupils flared. It was as if the climax were filling her with opium. Her lover lunged with a ferocity that made the headboard slam against the wall. Euphorically, he groaned that this was what she wanted: "*Voici ce que tu veux*."

Animal. That's what he was. Adrienne had never seen a man's sex before, but she felt certain that her neighbor's was unusually substantial. He's like a horse, she thought to herself. A stallion, *un étalon*. And Adrienne could not work out why such a thought should make her burn.

She spied on the lovers until her neighbor's thrusts grew fiercer, and, with his every lunge, she could hear the wetness of the woman's sex. Adrienne imagined his sex inside her own—its length, its savage intensity—and as she did so, her fingers caressed her breasts through her thin, summer blouse, making her nipples even harder than before. Once she'd started, she couldn't stop. She felt like her body might explode with wanting, but Adrienne had never allowed herself to orgasm before, so she kept the floodgates strong. Having steadfastly blocked out her every sexual need since she was a girl, she was no stranger to control, yet here, watching, at the age of twenty-one, she longed to let go. Soon, her own caresses sank lower, finding the crease of her sex through her skirt. *He's like a pig*, she thought, as she caressed herself. *It's his fault I'm behaving in this bestial way. He's polluted me, invaded me, this man who does not smile and performs like a stallion.*

She brought herself to the very edge of ecstasy, falling against the doorjamb and whimpering with need. But quivering there, her fingers glued against the shape of her sex, she dared not permit herself that final joy.

What would she become if she did?

Instead, she snuck away into the night, abandoning her body and all its needs as if it were a dream.

The following night, she watched again. This time, he was with a woman who had a deep, golden tan, and a pair of large, voluptuous breasts. So big were these breasts as the woman lay on the bare boards of his apartment that Adrienne couldn't glance away. Those breasts were as big as the woman's head. On recognizing this, Adrienne gasped, as if she knew danger was near.

Adrienne's neighbor, *L'Étalon*, stood astride the woman, his sex prostrate in his fist. He was moaning loudly as if he were inside her. "*Laisse-moi faire*," he groaned through those savage teeth. "Tell me I can do it." His green eyes flashed.

"I've been asked by so many," said the woman, caressing her breasts. She lifted them with both her hands, watching them with amazement as if she'd never seen them before. "I've never said yes to such a request. I simply *couldn't*. It's degrading, you know? I'm not that sort of girl."

"*Laisse-moi*," he growled. "It is what you need."

"Or what you need," said the woman, sharply.

The Stallion, *L'Étalon*, gave a dark, crooked smile.

At this, Adrienne had to smother a whimper of need, because she knew she'd give this bestial man whatever he wanted—that's how dangerous he was. She was already touching herself through her sheer summer dress. A few minutes earlier, when she'd first arrived home, she'd removed her underwear because she'd dirtied it so much by thinking of *L'Étalon* —how big he was, how cruel, how he'd hurt her if he entered her. As she caressed herself now, she felt a strange little bud between the naked folds of her sex—it was hard and wet and desperate. Before, she'd always considered her sex to be delicate and smooth.

"I'm going to do it," growled the Stallion, a snarl on his face as he glared down at his lover. "And you'll not stop me."

With that, he released a stream of urine onto his lover's breasts, hitting them with the noise of water pouring onto tiles. He groaned in ecstasy, as her breasts gleamed beneath the shower. The woman let out a squeal of amazement that sounded far more ecstatic than it should, and Adrienne had to stop her own ministrations for she was too shocked to carry on. But even as she pulled her fingers away, she felt a sudden current of pleasure that shot through her sex, making her tumble backwards. Automatically, her treacherous fingers pressed themselves back on that swollen bud, kneading out the final shots of joy. By the time she was done and breathless, she realized she'd been mewing with pleasure. Surely *L'Étalon* and his lover had heard!

She raced back to her own apartment, ashamed and terrified, *L'Étalon*'s deep groans ringing in her ears.

The next morning on the stairs, Adrienne met him. She was on her way to work and he was coming up with a bottle of milk. He was wearing an open shirt and was unshaven. His green eyes were shining, intense. As she made to pass him, her pulse beating like a frantic bird, he grabbed hold of her and pushed her against the wall. His grip was carnal, his body hot and firm. He smelled of clove cigarettes. Already, she felt a surge between her thighs. He put his lips to her ear. "The other day," he said, "I was reading in the park when I promise when I'm done with you, you will feel the same."

He was gripping her shoulders hard and his knee pressed against hers, his thigh nudging at her sex. She felt the damp pleasure again, burning there, so plentiful that it felt like she had wet herself. It was insistent, this pleasure. She almost couldn't keep it back. It quivered, barely controllable, threatening her with ecstasy thanks to the abominable story he had told, and the fact that he was grasping her, against her will.

She felt a deep, ecstatic shame.

At her ear again, he murmured, "What do I remind you of?"

She gasped that she didn't understand—"*Je ne comprends pas*!"

"I always remind my lovers of something. For the woman I urinated on, I reminded her of a filthy child that pulls the legs off spiders and fries ants under a glass. What am I for you?"

"An animal," she whispered.

"What sort?"

"The stallion! *L'Étalon*!"

This admission thrilled her needy sex.

He ran his warm fingertips along the edge of her jaw. "You want to be taken by a stallion," he murmured, his lips so close to hers that she could taste his hot breath. "A vast horse with an enormous penis as hard as steel. An animal of such virile bestiality that it would take you in a storm. Relentless, it would be. No thought of your needs, only the will to sate its own."

The orgasm took her so deeply that she cried out as if she'd been plundered by it. When, eventually, it released her, she was trembling and changed. She had given way. She had become *a thing*.

L'Étalon had cupped her breast. Her nipple was so hard that it hurt. Slowly, he smiled.

But it wasn't the smile of the merciful or happy—it was the crooked smile of the adder. It made his eyes darken, and as he walked away, her heart darkened too.

That week, *L'Étalon* kept his door firmly shut. She did not see him. So she let the butcher's son take her. He, after all, seemed a safe sort of man. He took her on the beach where the sand was still hot from the sun, her arms spread-eagled as he thrust his hard sex into her, burying her deeper and deeper into the shore. She'd thought the first time would hurt more than it did and felt disappointed by that lack of pain. He was big, but nowhere near the size of *L'Étalon*. She needed the Stallion's size, rigidity, and sheer ferocity. As the butcher's son thrust into her, she felt no shame. *L'Étalon* had taught her she was beyond it.

"You beast!" she cried out to the butcher's son, willing him to be rough as he thrust himself inside her. As soon as she'd said it, his pace grew urgent. "*Tu es L'Étalon*!" she gasped again, and immediately the orgasm threatened. For a split second, she considered what it would be like to be taken by a horse—the sheer strength of the beast, the rippling of its muscles, the aggression, the frenzy, the impossible size. She would be pinned down, taken, robbed, treated as an object of unstoppable pleasure. She didn't see any difference between such a horse and the stranger who lived opposite her—the neighbor she hadn't seen since their meeting on the stairs. Just to think of him, of *L'Étalon*, made her depths desperate to yield.

But she could not permit it.

Only *L'Étalon* should have her.

The butcher's son's spasm was so deep that it forced his sex even further into her, driving him to ecstasy as his hand trembled on her breast.

"*Oh cherie*," he hissed in her ear, as he collapsed on her afterwards, panting like a dog that's raced too far.

She said nothing as she stroked his hair.

She felt strangely empty.

That week, she had sex with others too. An artist took her in his shack by the sea, lunging into her with such sudden depth that she almost felt the orgasm straight away—he was a beast so penetrating that she could do nothing but yield. He was hard, muscular, his body thick and sweating. "*L'Étalon*!" she cried out.

In a flash, she remembered *L'Étalon* standing over his lover's breasts and unleashing the golden shower. No sooner had Adrienne recalled this than she gave way to a pleasure greater than any she'd felt.

The following weekend, there was a knocking on her door early in the morning. She had taken to sleeping naked, her body pressed against the cool sheets in an attempt to cool her savage flames, so she pulled on her robe and went to answer. There stood the stallion, his trousers unbuttoned, his stiff sex wielded in his hand. When she saw this, she gasped and fell sideways against the doorjamb, trying to support herself as she stared at his bare sex. But he pulled her against him, putting his lips to her ear. "Those who crave the stallion, want extremes," he said. With one hand, he grasped her throat just tightly enough that she felt it. She grew dizzy, but not from lack of breath—his words had made things spin. "When I was a boy," he told her, "I almost hanged myself."

She jolted with need.

He explained how he'd tied a rope to an overhead beam and had stood on his little bed and made a noose for himself. "I wanted to make my mother sorry," he said. "I wanted to imagine I was gone and that she wished she had treated me better. But as I balanced naked at the end of my bed, ready to leap and let myself swing, I felt my sex grow so hard that I immediately came. To watch the seed shoot from me so powerfully was like watching my soul fly from my body. I flung forward as ecstasy roared inside me, and at that, I felt another, yet deeper spasm. You see, in a way I died that day. Since then, I've lived only for sex."

On hearing this, she was in such a frenzy that a wet, spreading pleasure radiated from her depths, making her flush with desire. She was hot and quivering. "Take me!" she pleaded. "Others have done so, but none of them are you."

Still holding her by the throat, he thrust his free hand under her robe and grasped her bare sex.

"Please!" she cried, thrusting into his hand.

Without thinking, she had grasped his own naked sex, which required her to use her whole fist. Suddenly aware of its stiffness and size, she gasped, faint with need. She thought she smelled smoke and the skin of hot strangers…but perhaps that was just her desire's illusion.

"First," he said, "I wish to see you taken by men who are not as large as I. I must see you used as if you are an object. Come now."

"I must wash," she gasped.

"Be bestial," he said.

Just like that, her sex palpitated, as if already filled. She nodded as she bit her lip.

He led her to his flat.

His room was full of silent smoking men. Eight of them in total. Their eyes crept towards her, before assessing her body. From behind her, the stallion slid the gown from her shoulders, unwrapping her, the prize. She stood before them entirely naked and trembling. They watched her with interest, their eyes wandering over her body. She saw they were hard inside their trousers and this excited her.

L'Étalon grasped her arm and pulled her roughly towards the bed. There he had a ruddy-faced man hold her down, while he, *L'Étalon*, bound her wrists with a silk scarf. It hurt to be tied this way. She found herself writhing with longing. If he asked her to go, if he set her free, she felt her every hope would die. She was afraid to experience the depths of true pleasure, yet she'd never felt this alive.

"Please!" she cried.

L'Étalon stood back and watched, his hand wielding his sturdy sex—a sex bigger than any she could imagine, a truly *equine* sex. To own such size made him seem beyond human. A golden, bestial god. His green eyes smoldered. "We are your guards," he said, "and you are our prisoner. Take every one of us inside you 'til we're satisfied and we will set you free."

She made a noise inside her throat that she'd never before made. It was grateful, ecstatic, and shocked. Her heart palpitated inside her chest and her body arched and writhed, as if it knew its duty.

She parted her knees, rolled her hips.

One by one, without removing their clothes, the men queued up, stroking themselves with lazy glee. Each climbed on top of her, spread her thighs, and penetrated her roughly, as if she were just a thing, *un objet*. They smelled of smoke, sweat, and breath. One smelled of menthol, another of cologne. Some had stubble. Others were smooth. Some grasped her hard, while others barely touched her. All manner of sex was thrust into her. Some were hard, some softer, some large, some small. The men growled and groaned, grunting as they thrust, sweating like pigs and lunging with such ferocity that the bedframe met their lust with its loud, lewd percussion. She gasped, strung like a bird, used and smothered, filled with streaming semen. The men's disregard for anything but their lust felt shameful and perfect and desperate and raw. Like *L'Étalon*, whose stare grew so fierce that it took on the gleam of lava, they had no regard for her feelings.

As they fell on top of her one by one, their sweaty bulk grinding and thrusting, she might have been nothing but a willing corpse defiled by hungry beasts. All the while, she stared at *L'Étalon* and his large, carnal sex. "None of them are like yours!" she gasped, as a soft-bodied man wrestled himself inside her.

L'Étalon's sex was an object.

The thought made her cry out.

After, as she lay defiled by all these men, her sex spread and stained, she felt absolutely free. She had almost earned her release from this prison. All that remained was *L'Étalon*.

He kneeled between her knees, raised her hips, and inch by inch, with a snarl on his lips, began to ease himself into her. She squealed at the insistent pain that told her she was free, and he pushed and pushed until he was halfway inside her. By then, she had stopped breathing. Her sex was convulsing with joy. "You are still like a virgin," he told her, those eyes bright and burning. With that, he thrust in further, filling her to the hilt, and she cried out at the glorious agony. Then he growled, "Now, for *L'Étalon*!" And at that, he fell on her, taking her ferociously, his muscles fierce with sweat and power, his speed as vigorous as a stallion's. Opening to this onslaught, she closed her eyes. In her mind, he was the horse with its hot, strong muscles and unparalleled sexual power. He thrust like a stallion with all of his being. The pain she felt and the pleasure were one. They seared through her, immense. She felt the ecstasy with her whole, trembling self, and suddenly her needs were no mystery any more.

It seemed that what she'd craved, all this time, was for a strong, relentless beast to penetrate her against her will; and for her to be so powerful that she'd gratefully, potently yield. ❖

Danica Davidson

Another Birth

They were down in the garden, where the air was perfumed with flowers and the little angel statues stared from behind spring-blossoming foliage, like Botticelli cherubs peeking out at the lives of mortals. It was not their home. It was a vacation home, and the writer thought it would be a good place for her to write. The house here was full of mirrors, of walls made of glass, like a crystal that allowed you to both survey the outer world from a safe distance and catch glimpses of yourself out of the corner of your eye. The writer's notebook was open before her on the patio table, the ink spilling like blood from an opened vein.

This story she was writing, based on parts of her life that needed telling, had been churning in her belly like a hunger. For years she had filled her diary, waiting for the day she would be mature enough as an artist to transfer her thoughts from a series of passages into a *roman fleuve*. She had gone into the underground depth of the subconscious and found her way back out with Ariadne's thread, and the story followed, wanting to be told. It was then knitting together the bones of a book as her head moved with the heat of wine but the precision of a doctor's scalpel, finding the best ways to write it all down. When she wrote at night, the moon bathed her into a silver statue, a woman statue to offset all the little angels.

Yet now, as she was rushing the words out into the notebook like blood, birthing the story, she became aware of her lover sitting across from her, watching her more keenly than the statues. His eyes were as intense as a Minotaur's, something primal driving in his emotions, something from the deep forests of the unconscious. Suddenly the perfume of the flowers choked her and her pen stilled, because she knew the look in those eyes. She already knew what he was going to say.

"You create so many stories," he said. "Let us create something together."

She veered back against the idea. All her life she had escaped into words like labyrinths, first in the books of others (the sweet smell of the library, of comforting dust and old pages like friendships) and then into her diaries and finally her books. Her blood was ink and she was pregnant with stories. But she knew he wanted them to have a physical pregnancy, so that together they could have a child. She did not understand how a man she loved, a man she thought she knew so well, could put this chasm between them, could not understand her.

She had heard it many times, that writing a book was like experiencing a pregnancy, and yet writing roiled like a pleasant heat of a spa, sometimes scorching but always so healing, so that it always ended in a blissful, cathartic warmth. The thought of an actual, physical pregnancy repulsed her. It would take over her body, to pull at it like the moon pulls waves, dragging her into the undertow. The very notion of sharing her body for a pregnancy was like opening herself up like a hotel to whomever might show up. The man could not understand this reaction she had, and he loved her and vowed to be with her and the child. She could not explain to him that it was impossible, a pregnancy. She could not explain to other women that it was impossible, women who came to visit her with babies hanging on their hips or peering behind their skirts with teacup eyes. If she became a mother, she was convinced, her stories would leave her, her veins fill with blood instead of ink. A pregnancy could only be creative and wonderful if a woman chose to have one; but for her, who so resisted the idea of motherhood over art, it would make her a victim of her own body's ability to cage her.

"I cannot," she said, and even though she was a writer, she found herself voiceless in explaining to him. The cherubs were staring at her now, looking like little children. She ran into the house and found herself surrounded by the crystal mirrors, and she caught the sight of her face, pale from the argument. Her ink-stained hands were trembling. She could see him still out there in the garden, his head tilted down, his face away from her and the mirrors. There were no words to breach this gap. When she walked to the glass window to call to him, she did not see it until she ran into the pane. When she looked at her hand where it had been hit, there was a ruby gemstone of blood. She looked around and realized she was in another labyrinth now. ❖

Chrissi Sepe

Caramel Macchiatos and Conversation

"What I pursue, which others do not believe in, has often materialized."
—Anaïs Nin, Mirages

I dream there is an upright, five-inch tall, lizard loose in our house. It is a problem. At first, he is stuck to my sister's face, but she is not aware. I am horrified. He jumps off and is somewhere else in the house. We cannot catch him. My mother tries, but she can't catch him. He goes to different spots in the house. Finally, my father who, for some reason, is alive and healthy finds the lizard and gently picks him up by putting one hand at the top of the lizard's head and the other hand to support his bottom. He removes him from the house permanently. I feel so much better now. Dad has come to the rescue.

I watch the top of your head while you read my notes. Your eyes never leave the paper while you slowly lift your coffee cup, sip the foam on top, then put it back down on the table. This is the end of the second week we've met at this same coffee shop, and I wonder if you've been keeping track of the days as I have. I still can't believe you hired me to help you write these stories. "I need a woman's point of view," you said. "Reminiscent of Anaïs Nin's style." I wonder if you are disappointed I'm not older and wasn't around at the time of Anaïs Nin's heyday in the early 1990s with "*Henry and June*?"

I know why you look so sad. Your novels sold well for twenty years, but lately, sales are slipping. This collection of romantic stories is your last hope to keep your publishing contract. Otherwise, as your agent says: "You and I will be on our own!"

Our twenty-year age difference is not so odd. Your girlfriend is ten years younger than you. I've only met her once. The day she surprised us while we were working at our usual table. I nearly spit out my Frappuccino when she came out of nowhere, hurrying to you, kissing and hugging you so warmly. I didn't even know you *had* a girlfriend! You'd never mentioned her. You never asked HER to write these stories with you! Yet just that quick glance has plagued my mind for the past two weeks. Suddenly, I am inadequate. I should have a tattoo on my forearm like she does. I should wear tighter t-shirts. My skin should be paler. My eyes should be blue. Everything I'd noticed about her in those few quick seconds I should have as she does. She's perfect to me because she has you.

You put my notes down and smile. "Wonderful," you say. It's your turn now, and you open your laptop to continue the section I wrote: "*I kiss the spot on your forehead right between your eyes. Gently, my lips barely touch the soft skin at the top of the bridge of your nose."*

I watch your large hands type as you squint into the computer screen. You turn it sideways so I can look: "*I kiss you there because I want to be the only person who ever kisses that spot on your face.*"

> *"I have never known the way we talk with anyone else. His answers are so close to my thoughts that we have the impression of hearing ourselves talk in the other."—Anaïs Nin, Mirages.*

We speak together with such ease. Even from our very first conversation, I feel I am talking to the male version of me. You are familiar. You tell me you feel it too. You have aroused my passion, but by awakening my passion, you have stirred up my jealousy. You freed the writer in me too. We trade stories. One afternoon, and one time only, you tell me about your girlfriend. "I have finally found someone I can relax with. No drama. I want someone who is just like me who never causes any problems." But life *is* a problem. Relationships are problems. You don't say you are in this relationship because you are madly in love. Do you think your girlfriend wants to know you are only with her because the situation you two share is the least troublesome you could find? If I were your girlfriend, I would want to believe you'd stay with me no matter WHAT trouble I caused you and that you were with me because you had passion for me. That you were with me because you loved me. Not because I was an uncomplicated piece of ass.

> *"I looked at his face and saw that he knew. I felt uncovered, happy, but hurt. Happy that he does know me, and terribly hurt that the one who comes so near to my thoughts and feelings should be the one I am not allowed to touch."—Anaïs Nin, Mirages*

Your best friend dies. It happens on the first afternoon of the third week we meet for coffee and stories. I tell you about my dad who died at the same age as your best friend. You tell me your girlfriend has never lost anyone close to her, that she's never grieved. I listen to you for three hours. I give you advice: "You never get better from the pain," I say. "But in time, you learn to live."

You try to avoid pain until you can no longer avoid it. All anyone really wants is to be understood.

On the fourth week, you stop answering my texts. I go to our coffee shop at our usual time just in case you are there but were too busy to answer. I wait for an hour. You never show up. I text you again for five days straight, and you never answer. But on the sixth day, you do.

Ahhhh—There's nothing that Caramel Macchiatos and conversation can't cure. I feel so much better now.

I dream I am in the audience watching you and another male writer trade verse line by line the way the old beat poets used to. It is your first live performance. I sit, but my feet don't reach the floor. I can barely sit still. I can't wait for the minutes to pass. I love hearing you two read—some rehearsed, some on the spot. But I am anxious and can hardly wait because after the show, I know we will leave together. We are a new couple. I can't wait for you to get off the stage so we can be together. I know my dream will be. ❖

Katie Doherty

Sky Bound

The light that radiates from the heart came out today; it said how happy it was and how enlightened it felt to be free from the restraints of pain. The mind started to work, word by word; day by day it became a whole and not just a ragged piece. Not sinew but a fully formed piece of flesh that had its very own working organs; it was Susie. She had fully formed for the first time since her birth.

Through the years she had been beaten, struck, torn apart, sewn together, unpicked, violated, penetrated and left to rot. Today she had been repaired, fed and watered and now she knew what true happiness was. She smiled again, allowing her teeth to see the sun; she opened her emerald eyes and her arms to a love she had never felt before. A strange yet familiar feeling, a new found confidence, self-love that she had never admitted to because every mouth put her down and made her feel like her birth was nothing but a mistake. A miscalculated occurrence. Trickery. A grave mistake.

The past few months had proved how low a being can come to edging their way to the end of their spirit, extinguishing that life candle and leaving this mortal coil by choice and not by the hands of disease or tragedy. She could choose how to go; creativity was her oyster and how she would be remembered would stand out from a death from natural causes, unlike most people—she had a choice. This was all so artificial though, from the mouths of medical professionals came the advice to take pills of power, pills of false hope and false happiness, that leading down the path to the promised land there was a chance that you could take a ride, face down on the train tracks, enjoy a bottle of alcohol with some painkillers or simply take a knife to your throat, to extinguish and to run away from living. They missed that part out of course and like a worker faced with redundancy Susie was frightened and unsure of her future; her life and meaning become redundant, and unlike the worker she could not find new employment—she just had to give up. Each day her head was heavy and her eyes were filled with tears. Alone in a room full of people, a carriage full of passengers, a street full of tourists—the only friends she had were those that lived in books and on records.

Words fell out of his mouth every day, good words, wonderful words, words that touched her heart but not her head. That headstrong feeling of hopelessness was something she had never felt before; she felt brainwashed and lost in a sea of doubts. Drowning each day, like a mermaid that had had her tail cruelly chopped off by an angry sailor, an old man with a pocket full of rocks. In one ear and out the other, they were just words, but she knew it came from a good place. He had a beautiful mouth, his lips perfectly formed, his teeth straight and his tongue was wise and funny—a beautiful being who was only doing what he thought best. The vessel that she once was defied all positivity, the darkness that fell within her filled her veins, her heart had blackened over the weeks, her bones became weak and her muscles tore as she cried. Her body ached continuously, and the days seemed long and pointless, she had decided to take time away from the bustle of living and enveloped herself in reading and the home, but she rattled around the house, lost and lonely as if she were the last living person on earth. As the sun went down she would paint a smile on her face as a showgirl would her ruby red lips, and as he came through the door to greet her she would smile and tell him about her wonderful day serving him food peppered with false happiness. She was a liar now. She only had the trust and support of those she had never met, through sensory penetration did she find her muse, her other parents and her savior—saved by those that inspired her to become who she truly wanted to be and make her realize that her mortality was worthy.

It all came to her one very dark morning as the train snaked its way through the underground tunnels; she sat, her head steeped in blackness, her eyes tired and red from thoughtful sleep. It was to be her last train ride, her last moment of human interaction, but something stopped her in her tracks. A young woman sat opposite her; her heart-shaped head intrigued her. She looked ethereal, ghost-like, childlike and so very beautiful; her frame was petite. so much hope sat in this small vessel, so many dreams and hopes, something she once owned and had somehow dropped, burnt and lost over the years she had lived, walked the path of life. It seemed rather ridiculous to give up now, her heart said no but her mind was the bully. This was the moment she knew that the poison was to be disposed of and she must continue alone, no matter what the next few days would bring. And so these days came upon her; like a warm summer's day she bathed in beauty, her smile wide and joyful. This wasn't how it panned out, however. The days were to become darker and more painful, she would lose sight of herself and others, her self-worth would become void and all she wanted to do was escape the pain she felt inside, the aching organs and the heavy bones she carried around. Day by day she had no idea how she would feel; one day she would be happy, another she would want to be like Ophelia before, floating down a river to a place of peace.

The first cut was the deepest, the conversation that was had with an educator, a person with the sole purpose to open the minds of children shot her down in an instant when she had a moment of pure creation; she felt her heart pound and her stomach flip as she felt she had discovered something, an alternative part of her mind that she wanted to use and develop. It was the excitement she had been looking for, but it was not academic enough—it was disregarded as truly ridiculous and she was dismissed like an unwanted foetus. Then she found her voice, her singing voice but this was dismissed too. From that moment on she found solitude in writing, a private practice that she never had to show anyone; she had no worry of criticism or incrimination—she could just be. It was to be her little secret. She had the galaxy inside her and no one was allowed to gaze upon it; the stars would burn until they burned themselves out; they would shoot around her body and they would shine brightly when she smiled, but this was just for her—it was the galaxy of Susie. In her adult life, this galaxy had long gone; it had dissipated and left her like a cruel lover, leaving her helpless and lost, always wondering what to do next. Traveling from one place to another, her bags had been packed more times than she could count on her fingers and her lack of roots had rendered her lost. She felt like she had died and her spirit was in limbo, it was between worlds, and she could never settle. When the spirit is tainted, when it is torn, it doesn't quite recover because it scars so deeply and you never quite forget what you have been through—it stays with you, it stains your memory and you will always hold it inside yourself from one place to the next. She often wondered how those who had been through horrendous catastrophes had appeared unscathed, but her conclusion was that they were also good liars, fabulous actors that would put Hollywood to shame.

And now she was sat in her own little space, her belongings around her or those that were left from many years of movement, remnants of her past lives pinned on the walls, stacked in piles and staring at her as she worked, as she wrote. She wanted her galaxy back. She wanted to feel herself bathed in the stars and her solitude to return where not a soul would ask her about what she was up to because, quite frankly, it was no one's business but her own. Her fragility begged for silence and simplicity. Her head begged for that surrealist mind she had all those years ago; she wanted to think only in texture, taste, feeling…she wanted to flip an idea on its side, upside down, eat it and watch it drop from the other side—she wanted Susie back, the true pure form that had been born all those years ago. Through this pain, how on earth could she bring this all back? How could she hold on to the string that connects to the childlike self she once was? It had been pulled over the years the farther she had strayed. She holds a child and an adult in her heart. but the child wants to reign supreme. Today she feels the child coming back slowly…ever so slowly… ❖

Steven Reigns

Poverty

When people talk of the poor
it is hard to look back
and think that is what I was.
It never struck me I was impoverished,
only decadent. The summer off
from school, no loan checks in the mail,
no off-season job in my seasonal Florida town.

I consumed Ramon noodles for weeks,
spent days reading Anaïs Nin in bed
with no air conditioning. Ceiling fan on high,
shuffling heat around my tiny room.

My walls were adorned with images of
Anaïs. I took library books to Kinkos,
photocopied her image, put them
in frames I bought at a thrift shop
and painted. Read of her living
on houseboat, buying a printing press,
and befriending artists.
It was during that summer
I learned decadence is
a state of mind and a life choice.

David Wilde

Duggans: I

life in space
the ace of spades
the digging for gold
the old and bold bad movies
modulating ancient modes
molds of special attention
given to speculation
ovulations of the
occult in two dimensions
are winning but
brief and lasting in
this clairvoyance this ambrosian
dream
and quick translation
to french or to
some francophone
flowing metallic grey
soup and green chile
automotive vehicular
traffic light stop just waiting
for green when we softly hit go
berta and me therapeutically reliving
our ambient dreams soothingly
catching those fleeting meme
moments around . . . of joy with
her coffee my tea her music
and my buzzing busy bee poetry—
her freckled nose (mentioned
before) in bloom before
this transformed
translation or metaphor

once before and since
we last spoke a year ago
when the café closed
locked and barred against
the rushing dashed impetus
of our meeting
and now another year
goes asunder—I wonder
is it a blunder?—or are we
just getting younger before
our time? (wishing she
could forgive and forget
the catholic church) or the
indiscretions of marriages
made in hurried public display
via the internet
a digital error of variable
multiplications a loss
of accountability—

across the street in
view of parking restrictions
the window seat of our cozy
corner table sets the mood for
shy self-conscious smiles—
remembering and looking
out to keep an eye on any
available spaces—questioning

our coffee table owner
the mystery man from
philadelphia watches our faces
—berta and me (again/voyeuristic)
the coming and goings and
naturally we just try to fill the
silences of the 12 years flown by
since berta's arrival here and even
try by listening all the while to the
gypsy melody this symphonic ode
to agree on an agenda christian
that is of a harmonious string
quartet-like pondering wondering
if it's smetana ma vlast she knows
that it's only the hiatus, a pause in her
chosen trajectory while beaming up
to the stars (a super nova?)

I know because I can feel
the heat of this explosion
this about to happen cosmic
energy a white dwarf or a red
supergiant suspended in space—
hovering!
It's not rocket science
turning the clock backwards
even romantically at duggans

on lead and yale the street corner
next to the lobo laundromat it's
also hard to miss.

the "children and animals" the
red dress, cold hands warm heart
consistent with blissful wishes
wishes of bliss make me happy—
not to miss your smiling face
and beaming healing presence
of course by innuendo not only
to new heights and unexpected
horizons a state of grace by
lingering here in suspended
animation the rondo sonata
of this space-age archipelago
arpeggios and french chromatic
even neapololitan cadences to
bridge the passage of our
non-relationship such as it is
potentially a lentern journey
homage to spring renewal—
a reason a step of faith a
friendship—beijos

Tuesday January 16th/
Saturday February 5th
(2016) 3:00 pm

Kennedy Gammage

The Apotheosis of Fat 1 and Fat 2

I

Once upon a time, in an average American household in a fairly large city, there lived two goldfish named Fat 1 and Fat 2. They lived in a fish tank in the living room, and were "part of the family," which also included a mommy, a daddy, a little boy and two cats. (Fortunately for these fish, the two cats did not seem at all interested in eating them.) Fat 1 was a beautiful golden orange color, while Fat 2 was a very striking pale albino fish.

These goldfish had been aptly named by the little boy (who had also named their predecessor goldfish, Door, though unfortunately Door had passed away some time earlier.) Even though they had been purchased at the pet store while small, Fat 1 and Fat 2 continued to eat their goldfish chow, and as time went on they became larger and larger until they were each several inches long and perhaps half an inch wide.

They lived in a tank with blue rocks on the floor, pieces of coral, sea shells and three brass peso coins from Mexico. There was also a bubbler to oxygenate the water, and a green plastic plant. When the tank was clean it was a very handsome little aquatic world, but as Fat 1 and Fat 2 continued to grow, the tank didn't stay clean for long. The dad had a boss who raised tropical fish, and the boss called the goldfish "pigs" for their voracious habits.

As they grew, the dad had to change the fishes' tank every other week, which became an onerous task. The water would become brown and unattractive, and a smaller fishbowl would have to be filled, de-chlorinated and let sit to achieve room temperature. Then Fat 1 and Fat 2 would have to be scooped-up and put in the fishbowl.

The heavy tank, weighing more than 50 pounds, would then have to be lugged (carefully) out the front door and dumped in the plants. Then the blue rocks would be dumped into a colander and rinsed out, and the tank scrubbed clean with soap and rinsed. Finally, the whole tank would have to be refilled, de-chlorinated, and repopulated with the fish. It was one of those thankless tasks that dads do which moms give little credit for, and it became apparent that it could not continue indefinitely.

It so happened that this family lived near a large urban park, and back before the dad got a lot fatter than Fat 1 and Fat 2 put together, he used to go jogging past the big reflecting pool in the park, which was full of koi and goldfish and turtles and water lilies. And one day the dad came up with a great plan: to release Fat 1 and Fat 2 into the wild!

One sunny Sunday, the dad, the mom and the little boy, whose name was Ben, put Fat 1 and Fat 2 into a large Ziplock bag, took them over to the park, and put the bag into the water of the reflecting pool. (Of course, you must always let the temperatures find equilibrium so that it doesn't shock the fish.) The family just sat there quietly, on the edge of the reflecting pool, enjoying the sunlight, and watching the crowd of people. It was a beautiful day in early fall.

At last it was time to release the fish. The bag zipped open, and first Fat 1 and then Fat 2 swam out into their new world.

II

Apotheosis may not be exactly the word I was looking for, but it will have to do. As my trusty Random House College Dictionary has it, apotheosis is "the glorification of a person, act, principle, etc., as an ideal."

What I mean by that is, Fat 1 and Fat 2 made a quantum leap into an ideal world. They went to heaven, and they didn't even have to die. They achieved Nirvana.

One day, Fat 1 and Fat 2 were living in a cramped and dirty fish tank, which was only truly clean twice a month, and at all other times was becoming increasingly polluted with their own filth; through no fault of their own, I might add. They were just big fish in a small pond.

Then on that fateful day, they swam out into a perfect world, an aquatic realm filled with light, glowing green and beautiful with sunlight, a realm many orders of magnitude larger and more ideal than their tank.

It really struck me at the time that they had made a great leap that day, and that it was somehow metaphoric for the spiritual transformation that the saintly few had been reputed to achieve throughout history. I am thinking of someone like Paramahansa Yogananda. I'm not comparing my fish with Jesus, though I know that was His symbol...

I also felt good because I had done them a favor. An almost unthinkably big favor, even though it was a little thing.

The coda to the story was, a few weeks later I was jogging by the pool and I saw Fat 2! Being an albino, she was easy to spot – she'd managed to avoid the great blue heron that roosts on top of the Botanical Building, and finds her kind so delicious. There you have it—they'd made the great leap, and life was good.

III

Of course, light is an important factor in the story. I think what made such a strong impression on me the day we released the fish was the sparkling light in the reflecting pool. If it had been a cloudy day I might not be writing this.

I thought about this yesterday afternoon after work, when I was walking down the side of my house towards Upas Street. The sun was still out, and it was the golden hour, perhaps half an hour before sunset. A jogger was running along the dirt path across the street, in front of Boy Scout headquarters, and she was brilliantly lit and running into the light. It made me think of the apotheosis of the fish, but of course all this woman was doing was jogging. To her it may have been no big deal. Maybe she was squinting and cursing the light—who knows? But to me it was a beatific vision: glowing, she ran into the light.

IV

What would it take for a person to make a transformation like that? What if they didn't have to transform at all? Perhaps all they would need to do would be to change the way they look at the world. (Of course, the fish were in a physical cage, and had to be moved, but we carry these possibilities inside us. We don't necessarily have to move to change.) What if we are all in a perceptual cage, with some clear days but mostly obscured to one degree or another by our own negativity?

It was Blake who said: "He who sees the Infinite in all things, sees God." He also said: "If the doors of perception were cleansed, everything will appear to man as it is, infinite." Which of course led to the cleansing efforts of Aldous Huxley, as well as the musical stylings of Jim Morrison and The Doors.

I don't know about seeing the infinite in all things: that sounds difficult. But I know at least one way to see the infinite. Look up into the night sky. Preferably the dark, dark moonless night of the country. The long, disk-like expanse of the Milky Way places us within our own (impossibly gargantuan) galaxy, and beyond that... Let your mind wander those dark paths, farther out and further back in time, progressing towards the infinite.

Will this make you a better person? Maybe yes, maybe no, but I'll bet Blake would applaud your efforts. After all, the ancients saw gods out there: gods, monsters and mythic heroes. At the very least we see great beauty, and evidence of the infinite.

So I rephrase the question: what can we learn from the apotheosis of Fat 1 and Fat 2? That there exists the potential for joy? That there is beauty in both light and darkness? That sometimes our own self-interest can lead to a greater good?

V

One day I read in the paper that there had been an act of urban terrorism in the park. Someone had poisoned the water of the reflecting pool, killing the fish. The next time I jogged past, the pool had been drained, and yellow "keep out" tape had been installed around the perimeter. Though denial was still an option, it appeared that Fat 1 and Fat 2 were dead.

This made me sad, of course, but I also realized that the fish had probably enjoyed many months of freedom in their perfect world, and everyone knows that nothing lives forever. Even the mountains are worn down by the wind and the rain. They rise and fall in geologic time as we rise and fall in ours.

So I guess that "perfect world" wasn't perfect after all, and of course it wasn't. It was just a pond in a park, a place for ducks to drop in during their migrations. That glowing jogger wasn't perfect either, and neither am I.

We are all like Fat 1 and Fat 2, just living our lives. If you happen to land in a lovely, light-filled place, try to enjoy it while you can.

Changming Yuan

Poems

Summer Stream

With all the transparent secrets
            Of the last ice age
(Or beyond the atmosphere)
You keep flowing
                        Towards the sea
            Leaving all wildness behind
Along your two vast banks

Missing

Your presence will fall upon me

Like the first rain
            Of spring, and
Everywhere I go
            Is mushroomed
With its song

Cheese, Vancouver in May

Don't even think of
Trying to pretend, but
Just show your most natural
Charm and grace; stand straight
Amidst the greening maple trees
Hold all the blooming cherry flowers
Closer to your heart; face towards
The bluest sky above the pacific
Move a bit more forward
Before the grouse mountain
Shake off the rain drops of last long winter
On your hair, and

Say cheese, you vancouver in may

Harry Kiakis

The Room of Forgetfulness

The Room of Forgetfulness
contains castoff totems and taboos
and a trocadero of delights.

All forgetfulness in life's raging torrent.
But pent-up Karmas in that Room
have not forgotten. How could they?

In some barbaric dawn
the door will be breached.
With a silent whoosh
a delicate tapestry, shot thru
with will and forgiveness,
passing by Dante in a safari jacket.
Levant handing out tinsel stars,
pervades this tiny universe.
Bounding and rebounding with all
Karma, leading to destinations unknown.

Items of Interest

A Unique Approach

A review of *Anaïs Nin: An Unprofessional Study* by Kazim Ali
(2017, Agape Editions, 184 pp.)

> *"In an interview with the East West Journal, she says, 'my ideal would be a page of writing which would be like a page of music. There must be a language, a way of expressing things, which bypasses the intellect and goes straight to the emotions. I want to evoke the same reaction to writing that I have to music.'"*

Kazim Ali entices all varieties of Anaïs Nin-intrigued readers into the mellifluous poetic prose of this befittingly extraordinary exploration of Nin's literary fiction. *Anaïs Nin: An Unprofessional Study* is unconventional in the best sense of the word. It is not quite an academic piece, yet not quite biography, poetry, prose, or study guide either; rather, it takes us on a textual tango dance, leading readers in a staccato-pace with skirts drenched in unexpected insights. Ali re-enters the surrealist, psychological lands of Nin and orders them into a loosely thematic exploration, increasing the volume on movements, sounds, and colors.

Passages of the study are often unapologetically disjointed, abrupt, and abstract. As the study progresses, pages increasingly break up into one or two sentence-long paragraphs, as if the author has established such familiarity with the reader that he has deliberately cast-off the formalities of elaborate articulations and trusts us to float away on a leaf-boat traversing a stream of consciousness, or swimming in those oceans of pixel, immersed in the rich oils of a painting, subtly guided by his imaginative interpretations and the images gifted to us from Nin.

The study traverses Nin's novels via Ali's intuitive connections and associations of themes and characters. It flowingly positions us within geographies/localities (boats, houses, bodies of water, and galleries) and aesthetic journeys of Nin's work (paintings, dances, and music). In one of these fascinating chapters, we are carried through *A Spy in the House of Love* as it might be if rendered to film. Ali deftly continues on from Nin's vignettes and dreams up appropriate backgrounds, describes soundscapes, and directs our imaginative gaze into a series of scenes reimagined. These scenes are both faithfully recreated and filled in with the slightest splash of additional color, extending into the fabric of a new world—one of Ali's creation but birthed by Nin's influence. If Nin's scenes were, as sometimes accused, at times incomplete, (deliberately, according to Nin, in order to better illustrate the subconscious reality and thus invite our participation as readers), Ali takes up the pen and artfully adds his own touches.

Passages recount Nin's creative works in discussions of image and symbolism as they might be understood through related art and Nin's contemporaries. Ali contextualizes Nin's work by drawing from the world of artists, authors, and musicians whom she was influenced by and/or influenced. In another chapter, Ali takes us on a tour through the halls of a gallery of artworks, each paragraph an exhibit placard description of the media and scene from Nin's work, influences, or life.

Mixed media.

Soiled sheets mounted on stretchers. Should be soiled by the artist with bodily fluids of any kind; ideally involving other participants. All parties should be designated as creators of the piece in accompanying signage.

The inner cover of one of Nin's original diaries held in the UCLA collection displays two entwined pubic hairs carefully taped inside—those of Nin and her lover, Gonzalo Moré. From the pride with which Nin displayed this memento of her sexual exploits, the soiled sheets as an imagined artistic display seem salaciously appropriate for her stories.

Everyone embraces their own image of the iconic Anaïs Nin. This is true, not only for those who knew her personally and were familiar with different facets of Nin as she revealed them while living her many simultaneous lives, but also for the biographies and critical works or studies written by both strangers and friends. Scholars exploring Nin's work have often focused on their unique and subjective interpretations of her symbolic work, but Ali offers alternative vision rooted in his own artistic practice, while building on the established discussions of Nin's contribution to a (new) novel genre. Previously, Diane Richard-Allerdyce offered us a rigorous psychoanalytic exploration of *The Remaking of Self* in Nin's fiction, Bettina Knapp dedicated most of *Anaïs Nin* to probing the inner depths of the novels and short stories, Evelyn Hinz emphasized the presence of the subconscious in Nin's literary descriptions of reality in The Mirror and the Garden, and Sharon Spencer explored the symbolic water and of Nin's surrealism. Ali asks us to reconsider Nin's novel as seen by the poet, as postmodern work attempting to "enact in its form the experience it seeks to reveal" and inhabiting the space between poetry and prose, while contemplating the possibilities of such a genre as unbound from classic structure. The study leaves Nin's biography, diaries, and even her erotic fiction to one side, instead choosing to freely move through common threads within her novels, novellas, and short stories. Ali's unprofessional study, in turn, successfully "enact[s] in its form the experience it seeks to reveal," loosely structured on Nin's own critical writing and her first unprofessional study of D.H. Lawrence.

Utterly unique in its approach, pleasurable to read, and adding sonorous "waves of revelation" to a multilayered and creatively complex understanding of the brilliant literary works of Nin, *Anaïs Nin: An Unprofessional Study* is a worthwhile read.

—***Jessica Gilbey, PhD***

The Anaïs Nin Podcast, 2016 episodes (all found on iTunes)

Podcast 12: He Said, She Said: Anaïs Nin and Lanny Baldwin. Anaïs Nin wrote about her relationship with poet Lanny Baldwin in her diary, and until now we only knew her side of the story. A recently discovered memoir by Baldwin, however, tells a much different story.

Podcast 13: Music in Anaïs Nin's Life and Work. Anaïs Nin, coming from a musical family, not only embraced music, but incorporated it into her work. Listen to some of her favorite artists and learn what they meant to her.

Podcast 14: Anaïs Nin's Maternality with Jessica Gilbey. Australian scholar Jessica Gilbey discusses Anaïs Nin's relationship with her mother and how it informed the maternal in her life and her art.

Podcast 15: Anaïs Nin's Editor: John Ferrone. A look at Anaïs Nin's editor, John Ferrone, who has died at age 91, and how he affected Nin's literary canon.

Podcast 16: Anaïs Nin and Henry Miller with Barbara Kraft. Memoirist Barbara Kraft reflects on her intimate friendships with Anaïs Nin and Henry Miller at the end of their lives.

Podcast 17: Barbara Kraft Interviews Henry Miller. Barbara Kraft, author of the memoir *Henry Miller: The Last Days*, interviews Henry Miller in 1979.

Podcast 18: Anaïs: A Dance Opera with Cindy Shapiro. Los Angeles composer Cindy Shapiro discusses a new stage production based on the diaries of Anaïs Nin.

Podcast 19: Anaïs Nin's Family with Gayle Nin Rosenkrantz. Anaïs Nin's niece, Gayle Nin Rosenkrantz, reveals what it was like to be in the fascinating and complicated Nin family.

Podcast 20: Auletris: Anaïs Nin's Lost Erotica. The story of how an unknown collection of Anaïs Nin erotica was lost for nearly 70 years and then rediscovered.

Podcast 21: Auletris: Anaïs Nin's Lost Erotica, Part 2. A panel of experts—Rose Caraway, Anaín Bjorkquist, Lana Fox, and Jessica Gilbey—discuss the release of *Auletris*, the new Anaïs Nin erotica collection.

Podcast 22: How Anaïs Nin Was Censored by Amazon. The story of how Amazon, the world's largest retailer, made Anaïs Nin's *Auletris: Erotica* invisible to would-be readers.

Podcast 23: Anaïs Nin's First Published Diary and Its Characters. Anaïs Nin's unpublished 1965 diary presents behind-the-scenes revelations about the battle to include Henry Miller, Rebecca West and Nin's cousin Eduardo in her first published diary.

Durrell Library of Corfu Website (www.durrelllibrarycorfu.org)

The Durrell School of Corfu was founded in 2001-2, and flourished in its study-centre and library in Corfu until 2013, when erosion of financial support dictated its closure. During those years, we hosted twenty-four international seminars, on topics central to the interests of Lawrence Durrell (1912-1990) and Gerald Durrell (1925-1995): literature, the visual arts, science, zoology, ecology, and the history and culture of the Ionian islands. These included the "Gerald Durrell Weeks" in north-east Corfu, which continue under the aegis of the Durrell Wildlife Conservation Trust.

The Library of the Durrell School is now located in my house in the north of Corfu. While continued financial restrictions do not permit us to host meetings (but see below), the availability of the internet encouraged me, and a small number of voluntary colleagues) to establish a website for the Durrell Library of Corfu) which is extensively visited by hundreds of readers worldwide.

While I myself was an early and avid reader of Lawrence Durrell, and, following the first edition of my *Lawrence Durrell: the Mindscape* (1994), began to explore the idea of an ongoing seminar devoted to his work, it was Ian MacNiven who persuaded me that the school should be devoted to both brothers, especially since Corfu (where I had decided the school should be located) was home to them both in the years 1935-39. I followed that advice and the website of the Durrell Library of Corfu is dedicated as much to Gerald as to Lawrence, even though the scholarly literature directed at Lawrence is far more extensive. The Durrell Library of Corfu website follows this tradition.

The website at present has 16 sections

1 Our "**Mission statement**"

- to promulgate and facilitate study of the works and lives of Lawrence Durrell and Gerald Durrell and their families and associates. The term "associates" is extremely important because the Durrells were involved in so many ways with so many people in their work and in their friendships: pride of place must go to Theodore Stephanides, who was both a friend and collaborator to Lawrence and the mentor of Gerald, whose entire life and achievements are in large part due to Stephanides's influence during the Corfu years.
- to provide a forum for discussion of topics which were central to the work of Lawrence Durrell and Gerald Durrell.
- to provide a library service by responding to requests for information based on the Durrell Library. We are currently providing assistance to scholars in many parts of the world who value the unique resource of works by the Durrells and their

associates, and an extensive collection of theses, review articles, journals and manuscript facsimiles.

- to continue the work of our predecessor, the Durrell School of Corfu as a publisher.

In the latter case, we are proud to announce that in 2018 we will publish a scholarly edition of Lawrence Durrell's unpublished novel, *The Placebo: an Attic Comedy*, co-edited by Richard Pine and David Roessel, and published for the DLC by Colenso Press.

2 **News** – We publish any items of news, including notices of pending publications, events, awards and developments in Durrell studies.

3 **Notes, Queries and Comments** is available to anyone wishing to contribute a query, a brief note of information, or to stimulate a discussion on any aspect of the Durrells' lives and works.

4 **Reviews** features reviews of recent publications on Durrell-related subjects.

5 **Essays and Theses** presents the texts of essays and lectures on Durrell-related topics. It also contains abstracts of many theses on Lawrence Durrell and the full texts of some PhD theses.

6 **Biographies** – of Lawrence and Gerald Durrell, and of Theodore Stephanides.

7 **Corfu** – articles relating to Corfu (either during the time of the Durrells' residence here, or from a later period). Matters concerning tourism and the environment (including comments by both Lawrence and Gerald) are prominent in this section.

8 **Adaptations** – this section gives details of the three television adaptations (1988, 2005 and 2016-) of Gerald Durrell's *My Family and Other Animals*, and of the film version of *Justine* (Lawrence Durrell's *Alexandria Quartet* 1969) and his *Judith* (1965). The DLC holds copies of the film treatments of "Justine" by Joseph L Mankiewicz (1960) and Ivan Moffat (1967).

9 **Audio gallery** – sound recordings of Lawrence Durrell reading from his own works (poetry and prose) and the full version of his projected musical "Ulysses Come Back."

10 **Photo gallery** – photographs of members of the Durrell family and places associated with them.

11 **Video gallery** – films of otherwise inaccessible television programmes such as the BBC "Bookmark" programme *Lawrence Durrell – A Smile in the Mind's Eye* (1998) in which Richard Pine was the principal

interviewee and a programme consultant; and *The Garden of the Gods*, a 1966 film of Corfu made by Gerald Durrell.

12 **Publications for sale** – the Durrell School of Corfu published a total of five volumes under its own imprint (including *Judith* to mark Lawrence Durrell's centenary in 2012) and three more appeared under the imprint of Cambridge Scholars Publishing. Details of these, and other publications relating to the Durrells and to Greek literature, are included in this section.

13 **Bibliography** – this section at present concentrates on the bibliography of works by Lawrence Durrell and of books, articles and reviews dedicated to his work. It is continually updated.

14 **Textbooks** – presents the full texts of two basic textbooks on Lawrence Durrell:
- *Lawrence Durrell: the Mindscape* (1994/2005) by Richard Pine.
- *A Lawrence Durrell Chronology* by Brewster Chamberlin. This text is continually updated, as new information regarding Durrell's life and work becomes available.

15 **Library catalogue** – lists all books held previously by the Durrell School of Corfu and subsequent additions. It also contains a catalogue of facsimile articles and other materials by Lawrence Durrell and of review articles and book reviews on his work. It was a matter of deep regret that the closure of the School meant that this facility was no longer available to people living in Corfu, who frequented it. However, anyone wishing to borrow a book may contact us to make an appointment.

16 **Archive** – we have archived as much material as we have been able to retrieve of the activities and personnel of the Durrell School of Corfu.

In addition to our regular website activity, we will also have an event in October 2017: with the Ionian University (Department of Foreign Languages and Translation) we are hosting "Novel Encounters: celebrating Greek and Irish fiction writing"—a meeting of four Irish and four Greek novelists to discuss the general theme "Writing and Identity in a State of Crisis." The meeting will also include discussion of translations of and by Konstantin Theotoki and Theodore Stephanides. Details will be found on the website.

—Richard Pine

KAZIM ALI's books include poetry, fiction, essay, and hybrid form. He has translated books by Sohrab Sepehri, Ananda Devi and Marguerite Duras.

KASTOORI BARUA holds a Masters degree in English Literature from the University of Delhi. Her other interests include painting with various art media and watching Animé for its narrative and visual wonders. She lives in New Delhi, India.

SIMON DUBOIS BOUCHERAUD, a frequent contributor to these pages, teaches English and American Literature at the University of Nice, France. He did his thesis on Anaïs Nin and has lectured and written about her in several venues. He is currently working on a translation of Nancy Cunard's "Negro Anthology" and was recently hired to translate the libretto of Leonard Bernstein's "Wonderful Town."

DANICA DAVIDSON is a professional novelist and journalist who has been an avid Nin reader since high school. She's the author of the children's adventure novels *Escape from the Overworld* and *Attack on the Overworld*. Her art guide *Manga Art for Beginners* will be released in March and her children's novels *The Rise of Herobrine* and *Down Into the Nether* will be released in April and June, respectively.

KATIE DOHERTY is a bibliophile, storyteller, blogger and poet. She studied film at University, is a bit of a hermit and an avid collector of weird objects. She cites Anaïs Nin as her inspiration for writing fiction again.

LANA FOX is co-founder of Go Deeper Press. Her erotic books include *Cathedral of Furs: Ardent Erotica Inspired by Anaïs Nin*, *The Castle of Depravity* series, and the Amazon best-selling *Cream: An Erotic Romance*. She lives in Northampton, MA, with her partner Jacob Tavares. Find her online at lanafox.com or godeeperpress.com, or follow her on Twitter: @foxlana.

KENNEDY GAMMAGE majored in English at U.C. Berkeley. He resides in San Diego, and his personal website is www.travelogorrhea.com. He has been published in *A Café in Space*, *SN Review*, *Deus Loci*, and *The San Diego Poetry Annual*.

JESSICA GILBEY was awarded a PhD for her thesis titled *A mother (A)Rosa: Anaïs Nin and Reconceiving Subjective Birth* in 2016. She is an enthusiastic Australian wordsmithstress and her blog *Poetrianais: Milky Wor(l)ds & Wishes Whirled* can be found at https://poetrianais.wordpress.com. Jessica possesses an endless appetite for all things poetic, feminine, and salacious. You can connect with her on Twitter @Poetrianais.

HARRY KIAKIS joined the Army at age 17 and served in Korea and Japan. He went on to graduate from Brown University. He and his wife Connie got to know Henry Miller. Kiakis kept a candid journal of the times they spent with Miller, at one point living in his home while Miller was in France for the Summer. His journal was recently published: *Henry Miller in Pacific Palisades*.

CASANDRA LIM received her B.A. in English and Political Science from the University of Connecticut and her J.D. from the University of Connecticut School of Law, where she was a member of the *Connecticut Public Interest Law Journal*. She is licensed to practice law in Connecticut and Florida. She lives in Connecticut where she works full-time at an insurance company and part-time as an Adjunct Professor of English at Goodwin College.

JEAN OWEN obtained her PhD in 2013. She is now a freelance researcher and writer based in London. Jean's interests lie in feminist theory, incest studies, psychoanalysis, anthropology, narrative traditions, and first-person writing. She has published articles on Anaïs Nin and Kathryn Harrison and is currently writing a book on daughter-led incest narratives. She is also working on a novel titled *Salt*.

RICHARD PINE is the author of *Lawrence Durrell: the Mindscape* and of works on Oscar Wilde, Brian Friel, post-colonial literature, music and broadcasting. His most recent book is *Greece Through Irish Eyes* (2015). He is a guest lecturer at the Ionian University in Corfu, a regular columnist on Greek affairs for *The Irish Times*, an obituarist for *The Guardian* and writes programme-notes for the National Symphony Orchestra of Ireland. He is currently working on "Minor Mythologies: a student' s guide to popular literature and film," to be published by Cambridge Scholars Publishing in 2018.

TRISTINE RAINER was a friend of Anaïs Nin who co-taught a writing class with her for International College. She is author of *The New Diary* (1978) and *Your Life as Story* (1998). Rainer's TV movies include *Games Mother Never Taught You* (CBS), *Having It All* (ABC), *Secrets of a Married Man* (NBC) and *Forbidden Nights* (CBS). She is currently Director of the nonprofit Center for Autobiographic Studies (www.storyhelp.com).

STEVEN REIGNS is a Los Angeles-based poet, educator, and was appointed the first City Poet of West Hollywood. Alongside over a dozen chapbooks, he has published the collections *Inheritance* and *Your Dead Body is My Welcome Mat.* He holds a BA in Creative Writing from the University of South Florida, a Master of Clinical Psychology from Antioch University, and is a ten-time recipient of Los Angeles City's Department of Cultural Affairs' Artist in Residency Grant program. He edited *My Life is Poetry*, featuring his students in the first-ever autobiographical poetry workshop for LGBT seniors, and has taught writing workshops around the country to LGBT youth and people living with HIV. Visit him at www.stevenreigns.com.

CHRISSI SEPE is a novelist and musician who has studied writing and music in Canada and Boston, Massachusetts. She has published two literary novels, *Iggy Gorgess* and *Bliss, Bliss, Bliss*. Her essay *Anaïs Nin's Diary—A Recipe For Immortality* appears in volume 13 of *A Café in Space.* She currently lives in New York City and is working on her fourth novel in addition to flash fiction short stories.

COLETTE STANDISH is an English painter and photographer and a graduate from St Martin's School of Art, London UK. Colette has exhibited extensively throughout Europe and America. Her achievements include: Black and White Spider Photography Award, Hollywood, California 2016, Jessop's Photography Prize in London, 2000 and fellowship awards in New Mexico, Italy, and Spain. Her work is in many public and private collections, including the Museum of Fine Art in Santa Fe and the Anaïs Nin Foundation Art Collection. Colette published her first art and poetry book in 2010, *Viaggio: A Journey through Life.* Colette is a frequent contributor to this publication. In 2016, she won a competition to exhibit at Art Basel in Miami and is now represented by the Art Box Gallery, Zug, Switzerland. Colette is currently working on a new project, "Anaïs through the Looking Glass," and a project on the homeless.

DAVID WILDE is a Pushcart Award nominee for his poem "The Train" (volume 13 of this publication). Originally from the Rhondda Valleys of South Wales, he has been a resident of New Mexico since 1984 and an independent scholar at University of New Mexico. In 1993 a postcard from Lawrence Ferlinghetti stated: "Dear Wilde. You are quite mad or a genius in the wild." He is currently working on a biography of his uncle, artist Alfred Charles Slawson. Influences include Lawrence Durrell, Henry Miller and Anaïs Nin. He has been translated extensively in Portuguese and Spanish.

CHANGMING YUAN, 9-time Pushcart nominee and author of 7 chapbooks, started to learn English at age 19 and published monographs on translation before moving out of China. Currently, Changming edits *Poetry Pacific* with Allen Yuan in Vancouver, and has poetry appearing in *Best Canadian Poetry*, *BestNewPoemsOnline*, *Threepenny Review* and many others across 38 countries.

Publications by and about Anaïs Nin from Sky Blue Press

Auletris: Erotica (print, digital)

Mirages: The Unexpurgated Diary of Anaïs Nin, 1939-1947
(print: Swallow Press/Sky Blue Press; digital: Sky Blue Press)

The Quotable Anaïs Nin (print, digital)

The Portable Anaïs Nin (print, digital)

A Café in Space: The Anaïs Nin Literary Journal, Vols. 1-14
(print, digital)

The Winter of Artifice—Original 1939 Paris Edition (print, digital)

Anaïs Nin: The Last Days—A Memoir (Barbara Kraft; digital)

Anaïs Nin Character Dictionary and Index to Diary Excerpts
(Benjamin Franklin V; print, digital)

Anaïs Nin's Lost World: Paris in Words and Pictures, 1924-1939
(Britt Arenander; digital, soon to be in print. U.S. Edition)

DIGITAL:

D.H. Lawrence: An Unprofessional Study
House of Incest
The Winter of Artifice (1939)
Under a Glass Bell
Cities of the Interior:
Ladders to Fire
Children of the Albatross
The Four-Chambered Heart
A Spy in the House of Love
Seduction of the Minotaur
Collages
The Novel of the Future

ALSO:

Henry Miller: The Last Days (Barbara Kraft; print, digital)

FORTHCOMING:

Trapeze: The Unexpurgated Diary of Anaïs Nin, 1947-1955 (2017)

CPSIA information can be obtained
at www.ICGtesting.com
Printed in the USA
LVHW110937280419
615845LV00001B/178/P

9 780998 724614